Breadcakes for Breakfast

A Further 105 Devotional Readings

Gordon Kell

Scripture Truth Publications

Books by the same author

Footsteps in the Snow

When Angels Sat Down

Reader reviews of *Footsteps in the Snow*

"Thank you so much for … your daily posts. What a help and encouragement they have been throughout this challenging year!"

"How often the message every morning has been so appropriate to the difficulties which we have been experiencing."

"Thank you for your encouraging and sometimes challenging words... So often, they were just what we needed to hear that day!"

"The ministry the Lord has given you during this past year has drawn us closer to the Lord and to one another."

"Whether treading through the snow, joining Angels in worship, or now Breakfasting on the Bread of Life, Gordon's books have been a huge source of blessing to so many around the world via different media. The truths from God's Word, written in profound simplicity yet with a deep sense of understanding, coupled with so many personal experiences from his own upbringing, bring daily spiritual refreshment so lacking these days for both younger and older saints of every background.

They will continue to be mightily used of God; I wholeheartedly commend them to anyone who wants to know more of the Lord"

FIRST EDITION
FIRST PRINTING November 2024
ISBN: 978-1-917213-04-2 (paperback)
Copyright © 2024 Gordon Kell and Scripture Truth Publications
An STP publication

All rights reserved. No part of this publication may be reproduced, stored in a retrieval system, or transmitted, in any form or by any means, electronic, mechanical, photocopying, recording or otherwise without prior permission of Scripture Truth Publications.

Gordon Kell has asserted his right under the Copyright, Designs and Patents Act 1988 to be identified as author of this work.

Scripture quotations, unless otherwise indicated, are taken from the New King James Version®. Copyright © 1982 by Thomas Nelson, Inc. Used by permission. All rights reserved.

Spelling of quotations is that of the New King James Version British Text (formerly Revised Authorised Version), 1987.

Scripture quotations marked (ESV) are taken from The Holy Bible, English Standard Version® (ESV®) Copyright © 2001 by Crossway, a publishing ministry of Good News Publishers. All rights reserved.

Scripture quotations marked (AV) are taken from The Authorized (King James) Version. Rights in the Authorized Version are vested in the Crown. Reproduced by permission of the Crown's patentee, Cambridge University Press.

Scripture quotatons marked (NIV) are taken from THE HOLY BIBLE, NEW INTERNATIONAL VERSION®, NIV® Copyright © 1973, 1978, 1984, 2011 by Biblica, Inc.® Used by permission. All rights reserved worldwide.

Published by Scripture Truth Publications
31-33 Glover Street, Crewe, Cheshire, CW1 3LD

Scripture Truth is an imprint of Central Bible Hammond Trust Ltd, a charitable trust

Cover design by Gwyneth Duff
Typesetting by Helen Jones

This book is dedicated to Stephen Thomson, brother in Christ, and true friend.

List of Abbreviations

AV – Authorised (King James) Version

ESV – English Standard Version

NIV – New International Version

v. – verse

vv. – verses

Preface

Breadcakes for Breakfast is the third in a series of daily devotions. All these books are compiled from articles written from the beginning of the COVID period to the present day. They were first circulated amongst a small group of Christians during the isolation of lockdown to encourage readers and stimulate personal study of the Bible. Readers began to share them with other networks of friends and contacts in the UK and other countries, and the author was encouraged to publish them as books.

The first book in the series, *Footsteps in the Snow*, was released in December 2020, and the second, *When Angels Sat Down*, followed in March 2022. More recently, the articles have been translated into French and circulated widely in the Democratic Republic of the Congo.

The books are designed to be read day by day or simply opened at any page to find a self-contained reflection on a Bible passage. These bite-sized readings are intended to encourage Christians in their faith by reflecting on verses in the Old and New Testaments. There is a mixture of stand-alone, unconnected articles and of mini-series based on a biblical theme or character.

The articles in *Breadcakes for Breakfast* are intended to encourage readers to begin each day in God's presence. In John 21, Jesus invited His disciples to "Come and eat breakfast" (v.12). This illustrates that there is no better way to start each day than spiritually feeding on the Word of God, listening to the Saviour speak to our hearts and minds, thus preparing us to joyfully live out the life we have in Christ.

Contents

Introduction	13
Christ's obedience	15

Meditations on the Epistle to the Ephesians

God's will (Ephesians 1)	17
Praying in the will of God (Ephesians 1)	19
God's work (Ephesians 2)	21
God's wisdom (Ephesians 3)	23
Praying to know God (Ephesians 3)	25
Preaching in a barn	27
We will remember	29

The Holy Spirit

The Holy Spirit: Another helper	31
The Holy Spirit: Another teacher	33
The Holy Spirit: Another guide	35
The Holy Spirit: Another blesser	37
A jar of oil and a hand full of arrows	39
The silent power of a worthy walk	41
Walking in worship	43
Unity of the Spirit	45
The gifts to the Church	47
The building up of the Body	49
The power of a broken heart	51
The resolute heart	53
The transformed heart	55
The Lamb that was slain	57

Samuel

Samuel and Eli	59
Samuel and Israel	61

Samuel and rejection	63
Samuel and Saul	65
Samuel and David	67
The Gospel writers	69
The King of Glory	71
Announcing the Saviour	73
The voice of the Godhead	75
A cheerful giver	77
A cheerful worker	79
Loneliness	81
Instead of the lad	83
The joy of worship	85
Lifting up holy hands	87
The shortest verses and sayings	89

The simplicity of Sychar
The simplicity of Sychar: humility in witnessing	91
The simplicity of Sychar: patience and kindness in witnessing	93
The simplicity of Sychar: the focus of witnessing	95
The simplicity of Sychar: the joy of witnessing	97
Bethany, where heaven is open	99
Turning the world the right way up	101
Turning, serving and waiting	103

Spiritual blessings
Spiritual parenting	105
Spiritual shepherding	107
Spiritual home	109
Spiritual life	111
Sanctified life	113
The God of love…peace…all grace	115
God has chosen the weak things	117

Intergenerational togetherness: Abraham and Isaac   119

Prayer
The Lord's Prayer: worshipping, seeking, and thankful hearts   121
The Lord's Prayer: forgiving and protected hearts   123
Ceaseless prayer   125
A broken heart that re-built a city   127

Sight
Vision   129
Double vision   131
Cataracts   133
Short-sightedness   135
Far-sightedness   137
Tunnel vision   139
They saw His glory   141
Pressured vision   143

Shadrach, Meshach, Abed-Nego and Immanuel   145
My Church   147
Facing the uncertainty of the world in the certainty of
Christ's love   149
Seek those things above   151
It is written   153
Stay here and watch with Me   155
Life more abundant   157
Knowing Christ's power   159
The mountaintop   161
Fellowship and fruitfulness   163
Manna from heaven   165
Come aside   167
Rooted in love   169
Leaving the love of God   171
Coming to the Saviour   173
Fruit in old age   175

I hope in Him	177
God's faithfulness, living faith and focussed prayer	179
Building, praying, keeping and looking	181
The Name of Jesus	183

The Beatitudes

The poor in spirit	185
The mourners	187
The meek	189
The hungry	191
The merciful	193
The pure in heart	195
The peacemakers	197
The persecuted	199
Good soil	201

Abundant life

Twelve features of abundant life in Christ (1-6)	203
Twelve features of abundant life in Christ (7-12)	205
Ensuring we enjoy abundant life in Christ	207
Be anxious for nothing	209
A man of sorrows	211

The disciple's blessings

The disciple's Teacher: "Come to Me"	213
The disciple's rest	215
The disciple's yoke	217
The disciple's transformation	219
Psalm 1	221
Gold, silver and precious stones	223

About the author   225

Acknowledgements

The manuscript of *Breadcakes for Breakfast* was edited by John Broadley. Helen Jones prepared the layout and undertook the final proofreading. Gwyneth Duff designed the cover. I would like to acknowledge John, Helen and Gwyneth's considerable work and thank them for making this book possible.

Introduction

When I was a boy, I loved breakfast time. Every morning, my mother sent me to the bakery at the corner of our street to buy six freshly baked breadcakes. I can still feel their warmth as I carried them home. When I returned, mum would butter the cakes and give us one each. It was a breakfast I never tired of, and it sustained me all morning, especially if my sisters didn't feel hungry and I got two!! I have always liked the start of the day, and not just because of breakfast!

I love mornings and starting each day listening to God speak through His Word. As with David, my prayer is:

Cause me to hear Your lovingkindness in the morning.

In Psalm 143, despite the troubles he was facing, David teaches us the importance of going into the presence of God. Our inclination can often be to *talk to* God, or to discuss what He has said. David begins the day, not working out what he was going to do and how he was going do it, but by asking God to "cause" him to hear. He was asking to be prepared to listen. Sometimes we have already decided what we will do. We simply want God to bless our decisions. David was in crisis: it seemed time for him to take action to protect himself and build defences. But he appeals to God to "cause" or to "make" him hear.

I never liked long-distance running at school, but I enjoyed sprinting. It was over quicker! I was once chosen to run in a sprint relay race for my school at a district event, and I was to run last. As we got ready, my sports teacher took me to one side and said, "Gordon, I want you to run as fast as you can and don't look at the other runners – just look straight ahead." I obeyed my teacher to the letter, and as I crossed the line, I didn't know where the other runners were until the steward told me we had won the race. Throughout our lives, there are times not to speak, but to carefully listen and obey. We must never lose the wonder of the privilege of coming into the presence of God to listen. Jesus told Martha "one thing is necessary" and that Mary had chosen "the good portion" (Luke 10:42, ESV).

But what was David listening for? "Cause me to hear Your lovingkindness in the morning." God did not first teach David to know what to do. He taught Him about Himself, His lovingkindness. Our faith in God grows in proportion to our confidence in God's love for us. This enables us to trust Him: "For in You do I trust." And, in turn, God causes us "to know the way in which we should walk". David was brought into a place where he lifted his soul to God. If you read the whole Psalm, you will see David, like we often do, looking around at the real and present dangers which fill our souls with spiritual panic. David learned and had to relearn the importance of God making him "to lie down" (Psalm 23:2), "to be still" (Psalm 46:10) and "to hear". May God calm our hearts and spirits each day and cause us to hear His "lovingkindness in the morning" so that we can walk with Him throughout the day. I hope *Breadcakes for Breakfast* can help to stimulate this important aspect of the Christian life.

Note:

The articles each Sunday have a particular reference to the Lord's Supper (see Luke 22:19-20 and 1 Corinthians 11:23-26). This request, so important to the Saviour, was adhered to by the early Church on the first day of the week (see Acts 20:7). From this place of worship, we enter each new week in discipleship and service. By remembering Christ's love for us, we are inspired to serve Him, our fellow brother and sister in Christ and our neighbours, in love.

Day 1

Sunday

Christ's obedience

"Father forgive, them, for they do not know what they are doing."
(Luke 23:34, NIV)

"Father, into Your hands I commit My spirit."   *(Luke 23:46)*

Luke records the Lord's first words from the cross, "Father forgive, them, for they do not know what they are doing." He also records the last words, "Father, into Your hands I commit My spirit." It has always impressed me that the Lord's seven statements on the cross are embraced by the name of the Father. Everything the Lord did was in obedience to His Father. He said, "No one takes it (my life) from Me, but I lay it down of Myself. I have power to lay it down, and I have power to take it again. This command I have received from my Father" (John 10:18). It was a commandment requiring obedience. In His final statement from the cross the Lord Jesus fulfils the first part of the commandment. He lays down His life. It was man's intention to destroy the Son of God, but Scripture tells us He *gave* His life. He laid it down willingly, in obedience to His Father and in love for us. All man's hatred against God was seen in the crucifixion of the Son of God. But at the cross, Christ's love shone in all its glory. The Lord Jesus, in complete obedience to His Father, lays down His life. The cross is the most powerful demonstration of God's love. And Christ's obedience to death was the basis of God's power to save. This leads us to worship the One who loved us so much. It also teaches us the importance of obedience to the Lord in our own lives. It is how He can work powerfully through us. We cannot have powerful lives unless we have obedient lives. At the cross, we learn the greatness of God's love for us. It draws a response of love to the One who gave Himself for us:

> Love so amazing, so divine,
> Demands my soul, my life my all
> (Isaac Watts, 1674-1748).

The veil of the temple was torn from the top to the bottom. The veil was at the entrance of the Holiest of All. This was the place where God had dwelt amongst His people. The High Priest went into this place on the Day of Atonement. He sprinkled blood on the mercy seat to answer for the sins of the people. When Christ, the true sacrifice, died at Calvary, all God's righteous judgement against sin was met. The torn veil is a picture of how God removed the distance which existed between Himself and people because of sin. God appeals to everyone, based on His love – a love that has not changed.

There was a Christian who had a great interest in steam trains. He was invited to a factory where locomotives were made. The chief engineer gave him a guided tour, and took him to the department where the locomotives were designed. He explained the various stages of developing, constructing and testing the great machines. It was a fascinating day. At the end of the trip, the Christian thanked the chief engineer and shook him warmly by the hand. To his surprise, the man's hand was cold and limp. The chief engineer, seeing the surprise on the other's face, explained that when he was an apprentice, he had accidentally driven a nail through his hand. Ever since then, he had not been able to close it. The Christian looked into the man's face and said, "I have a Saviour who had nails driven through His hands 2,000 years ago, and ever since then He has never closed them to those who come to Him."

Day 2

Monday

God's will (Ephesians 1)

Having predestined us to adoption as sons by Jesus Christ to Himself, according to the good pleasure of His will. (Ephesians 1:5)

When I was a child I used to go to the Hull Fair every October. It was there I saw for the first time a pomegranate. This fruit always seems to be about to burst, as it is packed so tightly with its seeds. I am reminded how much the Holy Spirit fills the pages of the Bible with the blessings of God. This is certainly true in the first chapter of Paul's letter to the Ephesians, where we discover the manifold blessings of the will of God.

We often think of the will of God in terms of God's authority and power. But in the first chapter of Ephesians Paul brings before us the glory of God's will in terms of all the blessings His love and grace have determined. It was His will to bless us in the most astonishing ways. Paul was chosen as an apostle by the will of God and he lived in the reality of God's grace in his life, and the peace it had brought to his heart. God acted in grace towards us, producing peace in our hearts. It was this he wanted the saints at Ephesus, and us, to constantly experience (v. 2). He also wanted them to understand the immense spiritual blessings they had been brought into. These blessings are centred in Christ in glory. They are to be enjoyed now and we shall ultimately enjoy them in all their fulness in a future day. Paul explains how the will of God purposed us for blessing before the world began (v. 4) and how we have been accepted in the Beloved, that is, in Christ (vv. 5-6). God sees us through Christ and always acts towards us in the light of our position in our Saviour. Because of our failures we can confuse our spiritual state with our spiritual standing. God is never confused. He sees us in Christ. That doesn't mean He ignores our frailties, but addresses them in grace.

Towards the end of his life Paul describes himself as the chief of sinners. He never ceased to wonder at the fact that he was redeemed and forgiven (v. 7). God used him to teach us how we can be so far away from God, but by His love, His will and His grace we can be brought into all the nearness of sonship.

It is as God's children that we are made to understand the mystery of His will (v. 9) and the counsel of His will (v. 11). His purposes in Christ are unfolded to us and direct our lives. The Lord Jesus promised in John 10 that there would be one flock and one Shepherd. In verses 12 and 13 Paul states it was the Jews who first trusted in Christ and then Gentiles, like the Ephesians, also trusted. They were sealed with the Holy Spirit and formed into the Church. In Acts 20 Paul reminds the Ephesian elders to "take heed to yourselves and to all the flock, among which the Holy Spirit has made you overseers, to shepherd the church of God which He purchased with His own blood" (Acts 20:28). He speaks of this purchased possession in verse 14.

Then he turns to God with thankfulness and joy for the work of God in the lives of the Ephesian Christians, and he prays for their spiritual blessing (v. 16 ff.). It is a prayer that teaches us so much about spiritual growth and the power to live in the enjoyment of the blessings God has showered upon us.

Day 3

Tuesday

Praying in the will of God (Ephesians 1)

That the God of our Lord Jesus Christ, the Father of glory, may give to you the spirit of wisdom and revelation in the knowledge of Him. *(Ephesians 1:17)*

In Ephesians 1 Paul begins by writing about the power of God's will in determining our blessings in Christ. Then he lifts his heart to God in prayer (vv. 16-23). The work at Ephesus had begun is a small way in Acts 19, but had developed remarkably. Paul was writing from his imprisonment in Rome. He had had a report of the Ephesians' faith and love, and his heart was filled with unceasing thankfulness and prayer for them. Recently we have been reading in the Old Testament some long lists of names of people we know nothing about. But God recorded their names and knows absolutely everything about them. Never forget that, when we mention others in our prayers, sometimes knowing little about them, we bring their whole beings before God. Mentioning names in prayer is not a futile occupation, but a recognition of the greatness of God and His power to bless.

Paul's prayer was directed to the God of our Lord Jesus Christ and the Father of Glory. These titles remind us of the glory the Lord Jesus brought to God through His manhood, and also the response of the Father in glorifying His Son (vv. 20-23). Our prayers often focus on the practical needs we and others face from day-to-day. Paul teaches us to pray to deepen our knowledge of God. Everything else falls into place when we understand this primary need. Paul prayed that the Ephesian Christians would be given a spirit of wisdom, revelation, and enlightenment.

Spiritual wisdom is the practical application of spiritual knowledge which is imparted by revelation. Enlightenment opens our eyes to see and understand. Paul later deals with the practical aspects of the Christian life. But he conveyed in his prayer that the power to live practically for God comes from knowing Him. This spiritual relationship is developed through the ministry of the Holy Spirit in communion with Christ and the application of the word of God. Moses' face shone, and Stephen had a face like the face of an angel, because they had been in the presence of God. Paul's desire for the eyes of the Ephesian's hearts to be enlightened is illustrated by what happened to the disciples in Luke 24:31-34.

It is by communion with God that we grow in our understanding of our destiny in Christ (the hope of His calling). We also understand our preciousness to Christ (the riches of the glory of His inheritance in the saints). And we discover our power in Christ (the exceeding greatness of His power toward us who believe). Paul's prayer is thankful, focused and persistent. He prays for Christ to be glorified in our hearts and in the Church as a whole. He prays for a deepening knowledge of the resurrection, ascension and supremacy of Christ. Paul focuses on Christ's glory in verses 20-21 by presenting Christ's glory in His resurrection (the past), His ascension (the present) and His supremacy (the future). Christ is the Head of His Church. His people recognise His glory now and live in the power of it.

The apostle prayed for his fellow believers to enter into all the spiritual blessings we have in Christ. These blessings had shaped Paul into Christ's likeness and empowered him to serve and worship God. May we pray for the same spiritual outcomes in our lives and that of our fellow believers.

Day 4

Wednesday

God's work (Ephesians 2)

For we are His workmanship, created in Christ Jesus.

(Ephesians 2:10)

Ephesians 2 emphasises God's glorious work of salvation in Christ. Paul begins by reflecting on the past lives of his fellow Christians at Ephesus. Once, they had been controlled by the influences of the world and satanic power. These influences were evident in the idolatry that ruled their city (Acts 19). Their lives were engulfed in practices which were contrary to God and their own welfare, and would come under the judgement of God (vv. 1-3).

Then we read "But God..." God moved towards them in the richness of His mercy and the greatness of His love. Through the work of Christ in grace, He had taken them out of spiritual death and made them alive in Christ. There is a tremendous sense of the power of God's work in their salvation and its transformation of their lives. They were alive in Christ. Paul speaks to all our hearts in describing where we were in the past. He brings before us our position before God in Christ now. He also explains that this work of grace and kindness in all His people will one day be displayed throughout creation (vv. 4-7).

In the first chapters of the Bible we see God's work of creation. In Ephesians 2, we see God's work of redeeming grace. The physical creation was entirely the work of God. God's work of grace in the new creation is also entirely His. And the faith that brings us into this salvation is His gift. We are His workmanship created in Christ Jesus and enabled by Him to work out our salvation in lives of righteousness for His glory (vv. 8-10).

The Ephesians are reminded further of their history. They are described in the past as being aliens and strangers and of "having no hope and without God in the world" (v. 12). Then once more, Paul adds "But..." and writes the beautiful verse: "But now in Christ Jesus you who once were far off have been brought near by the blood of Christ" (v. 13). Christ is our peace. His work at Calvary brought us near to God and near to each other. Christ removed the wall of separation between Jew and Gentile. He formed His Church as one body through the cross. Jew and Gentile were responsible for the crucifixion of Jesus Christ. But on the cross, the Lord Jesus fulfilled the work of salvation, and through it preached peace to the Gentiles who were afar off and Jews who were near. Now we are made one and are citizens with the saints and members of the household of God. And by the one Spirit, we have access to the Father (vv. 11-19).

God's work continues in building His Church (vv. 20-22) as a holy temple in the Lord made, as Peter tells us, of "living stones" (1 Peter 2:5). It is a place where God dwells by the Holy Spirit. The Church is built on the foundation of Jesus Christ Himself, as the chief cornerstone, and also the ministry of the apostles and prophets. God works continuously in each of our lives and in the fellowship of His people to demonstrate His work of love, grace and mercy. We witness to this in our of worship of God, our oneness, our love for one another and by seeking to do good until the day when His Church is complete. In grace God works in us and through us.

Day 5

Thursday

God's wisdom (Ephesians 3)

To the intent that now the manifold wisdom of God might be made known by the church to the principalities and powers in the heavenly places. *(Ephesians 3:10)*

Paul was suffering imprisonment in Rome because of his ministry to the Gentiles. God, in His wisdom, chose Paul for this service. The apostle's Jewish credentials were outstanding. He seemed the ideal servant to be sent to his own people, and he served effectively among them. But God sent him beyond Israel into a world where idolatry was pervasive and dominant, and where Satan's power was so evident. Grace had transformed the apostle, and in Acts 9:15, when Saul was first brought to Christ, God explained to Ananias that Saul was "a chosen vessel of Mine to bear My name before Gentiles". It was this, called "the mystery" (v. 3), unknown in former generations, that was revealed by the Holy Spirit to apostles and prophets. After Paul's salvation in Acts 9, in the very next chapter Peter is sent to the Gentile household of Cornelius. And the mystery that the Gentiles would become fellow heirs, members of the body of Christ and partakers of the promises in Christ, began to be revealed. Christianity has been in Western Europe for such a long time that we forget how far we were away from God and how thankful we should be that He, in His wisdom, drew us to Christ.

Paul was chosen and empowered by God for this ministry. He had been the most dedicated and vicious persecutor of the Church. But the Lord Jesus transformed him. And he describes himself as "less than the least of all the saints". The world he served in was divided by language, boundaries, culture, religion, conflict, hatred, violence and hopelessness. In that world he preached the Gospel, manifesting God's love, grace and wisdom. Christ was building His Church, and the gates of Hades could not prevent it (Matthew 16:18). God had expressed His love and wisdom in the giving of His Son to make salvation possible. The Gospel removed all that separated people from God and from one another. Christ's Church was born and quickly grew. Paul had explained it is the dwelling place of God by the Spirit (ESV). By its worship, prayers, edification, preaching, righteousness, and its fellowship of love the manifold wisdom of God is seen.

God has accomplished in Christ Jesus, our Lord, His eternal purpose (v. 11). This is seen in time and ultimately in eternity (see Ephesians 5:27). It is through Christ that we have the boldness and liberty of access to the presence of God. Paul powerfully describes the journey which began when we were "without God and without hope in this world" and led us into a place of nearness to God and a hope in Christ that leads us into glory.

Paul comforts the Ephesian Christians, encouraging them not to lose heart because of his tribulations. This was the wisdom of God in action. Paul never doubted that all the circumstances he passed through would be used by God for His glory and the blessing of others. God in His wisdom took Paul to Rome. He was placed at the very centre of the most powerful nation on earth at that time to preach Christ Jesus "who became for us wisdom from God" (1 Corinthians 1:30). In doing so he encourages us not to lose heart but to "know that all things work together for good to those who love God" (Romans 8:28) and to rejoice in faith in the manifold wisdom of God.

Day 6

Friday

Praying to know God (Ephesians 3)

For this reason I bow my knees to the Father of our Lord Jesus Christ, from whom the whole family in heaven and earth is named, that He would grant you, according to the riches of His glory, to be strengthened with might through His Spirit in the inner man. (Ephesians 3:14-16)

You have a wonderful sense of the genuine care Paul had for the spiritual welfare of the saints in Ephesus. It was a care that extended beyond the ordinary needs of life and focused on the reality of knowing God and His love for them. He knew that this was the source of all blessing.

Paul addresses God as the Father of our Lord Jesus Christ. In doing so, he demonstrates what he had written in verses 11-12: "Christ Jesus our Lord, in whom we have boldness and access with confidence through faith in Him". In this confidence, he asks God to strengthen his fellow believers by the Holy Spirit in their inner spiritual man. The outward man ages, but the inner man is being renewed day by day (2 Corinthians 4:16). Then he prayed that Christ would dwell in the hearts of the Ephesians through their continuing faith in Him. They were "in Christ", rooted and grounded in His love, knowing both the security and peace of this position. We experience the love of Christ in fellowship with all the people of God. This enables us to begin to understand the vastness of the revelation of God.

When visiting the Swiss Alps, I have often looked up in amazement on dark winter nights at the stars which fill the sky. They are so far away, but they give us a sense of God's wondrous creation. A few years ago, I experienced, for the first time, virtual reality. The image I watched took me into space, and I felt I was walking like an astronaut amongst the planets in our solar system. It was amazing to have the feeling of being close to places like Venus and Mars. But I still had an abiding sense of the vastness of the heavens. This reminded me of what Paul was explaining. We already have experience of God's love, grace and mercy, and an understanding of His power and eternal purposes. God wants to deepen this experience and understanding of the unsearchable riches of Christ in fellowship with all His people. And, at the same time, to know the love of Christ, which passes knowledge. The Queen of Sheba was filled to overflowing by Solomon's glory. God wants to fill us with His fullness.

Paul conveys to us the immensity of the love of Christ and the riches of His grace. He also wants us to know the power of God to do exceedingly abundantly above all that we ask or think, through the Holy Spirit's work in us. The imprisoned apostle conveys most powerfully a spiritual liberty which could be contained by his restricted circumstances. He lived in the reality of the life he had in Christ who loved him. That love empowered his prayer for his fellow believers. Often our prayers are hesitant and limited, not because we doubt God, but because we doubt ourselves. When we begin to understand the vastness of the love Christ and all He has brought us into, we begin to pray with boldness and confidence. And like with Paul, God fills our hearts with worship: "to Him be glory in the church by Christ Jesus to all generations, forever and ever. Amen".

Day 7

Saturday

Preaching in a barn

Therefore those who were scattered went everywhere preaching the word.   *(Acts 8:4)*

An evangelist was cycling between two villages and it was a very warm day. As he cycled along, he saw a large barn in the field alongside the road he was travelling on. For some reason he felt the urge to preach the gospel in the barn. But then he thought … it was a warm day, he was tired and his mind was playing a trick on him. So he carried on. But as he travelled, the barn stayed in view and the compulsion to preach in it became stronger. At last he got off his bike and walked across the field and into the barn. Like most barns, there was a lot of hay and an absence of people. But to fulfil the urge to preach, he stood in the middle of the building and at the top of his voice shouted, "For God so loved the world that He gave His only begotten Son, that whoever believes in Him should not perish but have everlasting life" (John 3:16). Then he left the barn, got back on his bike and cycled on his way.

Some months later, he was preaching in a local church. He recounted his experience in the barn and told his listeners he couldn't understand why he felt God led him to go there and shout out John 3:16. After the meeting, he discovered why. A young man approached him and shook him warmly by the hand. He explained he had been working near the barn the evangelist had spoken about. On such a warm day, he had taken a nap in the hay. He was woken up by the words of John 3:16. The speaker had disappeared, but as well as waking up from sleep he had woken up spiritually and soon opened his heart to the Lord.

This incident gives us an insight into how, in the ordinariness of a journey, God can do something remarkable and lead us to the precise place He wants us to be. Most times it will not be a compulsion to visit a barn: it will, most probably, be in very commonplace circumstances. We have grown up with formal meetings in which the Gospel is communicated, and God continues to bless this ministry. But it has struck me afresh how the ministry of Christ and of the apostles was so often fulfilled by being actively engaged with people from all walks of life and in all the circumstances of life. The Lord sought and found beggars, and rulers of the synagogue. He was present at the joy of a wedding, and the sorrow of a funeral. He was inside houses, and outside in fields. The Lord Jesus was sensitive to every need. This same grace was evident in the Early Church and, strikingly, even persecution never restrained the Gospel, but only served to ensure its expansion.

So often we look for a special ministry and can overlook the opportunities everyday life provides. A Christian once said to an evangelist that he wished he could be an evangelist. The evangelist asked him what job he did and the man told him he had a market stall. Then the evangelist asked him how many people visited his stall; he explained he had lots of customers every day. The evangelist said it seemed to him that his friend already had a pulpit: he just needed to use it! This challenges all of us. And perhaps more than ever in the present circumstances, God would lead us to those whose hearts He wants to open to the Saviour: "And they went out and preached everywhere, the Lord working with them and confirming the word through the accompanying signs. Amen" (Mark 16:20).

Day 8

Sunday

We will remember

We will be glad and rejoice in you.
We will remember your love. (Song of Solomon 1:4)

I always think the opening verse of Dr T. E. Purdom's hymn fits so well with verse 4 of the first chapter of the Song of Solomon:

> Lord Jesus Christ, our Saviour Thou,
> With joy we worship Thee;
> We know Thou hast redeemed us,
> By dying on the tree.

We come into the presence of the Lord Jesus Christ, recognising the glory of His Person and knowing Him as our Saviour. As a result, joy and worship flood our hearts as we remember His redeeming love and the cost of our salvation.

The Lord has asked us to remember Him. He took from the table a simple loaf of bread and an ordinary cup of wine to describe the profound lowliness and amazing grace of His wonderful life laid down in death. Luke records the Lord's words, "This is My body which is given for you" and "This cup is the new covenant in My blood, which is shed for you" (Luke 22:19-20). The Lord Jesus focuses our hearts on the love that He has for us, and ensures that, even in the smallest groups, in the most constrained circumstances, and with the most simple things, we would always be able to "proclaim the Lord's death till He comes" (1 Corinthians 11:26).

We come together to remember the Lord and to express our gratitude to Him for His redeeming love. In the spirit of John 12 we 'make Him a supper'. But in doing this, we discover that it is the Lord who brings us into His presence to overwhelm us with His love:

> He brought me to the banqueting house,
> And his banner over me was love
> (Song of Solomon 2:4).

The banqueting house, or the "house of wine", is a vivid illustration of joy. The first sign of the Lord's ministry in John's Gospel was when the Lord changed water into wine at the wedding in Cana in John 2. Wine is used positively to express joy. In the parable of the Good Samaritan in Luke 10 the Samaritan poured into the man's wounds oil and wine. Over and over again in the New Testament, salvation is associated with joy. We have the experience of remembering the depths of the Lord's suffering for us and entering with Him into His joy.

In the final chapter of the Song of Solomon we are reminded that "love is as strong as death" and that "many waters cannot quench love" (8:6, 7). We look back to Calvary to see the depth of Christ's love for us. We look up to Him now in glory and are assured the flame of the Lord's love for us has never diminished.

We remember the Lord in the simplicity of His supper until He comes again. In that day we shall discover just how much the Lord loves us. In the meantime, may His glorious love transform and flow through our lives for His glory.

Day 9

Monday

The Holy Spirit: Another helper

And I will pray the Father, and He will give you another Helper, that He may abide with you forever. (John 14:16)

In promising the Holy Spirit, the Lord Jesus involves the whole of the Trinity. In John 14:16 it is God the Son who asks God the Father to send God the Spirit. This verse demonstrates the care that the Lord has for His people. He had been a constant help and comfort to the disciples in their lives, but He was about to go back to heaven. However, He was to leave them another Helper. The name 'Helper' or 'Consoler' is the Hebrew name given to the Messiah, and shows the closeness of the work of the Son of God and the Spirit of God.

The Lord speaks of "another Helper". Someone who would care for them as He had. The Father would send another Helper who would be with them in the future, just like the Lord had been with them on earth. And the relationship between the people of God and the Spirit of God was eternal. "He will abide with you forever." Once we are born of the Spirit, we are linked with Him forever.

Jesus then gives the Holy Spirit another name, "the Spirit of truth". At the beginning of chapter 14 Jesus said, "I am the way, the truth, and the life." Jesus is the way, and it is the Spirit who leads us to Christ. Jesus is the truth, and the Spirit is the Spirit of truth. Jesus is the life, and we are born of the Spirit. The work of the Spirit is entirely consistent with the work of Christ. However, the Spirit is only received and known by those who are Christ's. Of course, the Spirit has a powerful effect upon the world as we shall see, but here the Lord is explaining the relationship the people of God have with the Spirit of God. It is a twofold relationship. First, the Spirit of truth dwells with the whole of Christ's people, rather like the cloud and fire of God's presence in the Old Testament, which was with Israel as they travelled through the wilderness. But for the Christian, there is something else. The Spirit of truth also dwells in each one of us individually. This was what Jesus spoke of in John 7:38-39: "He who believes in Me, as the Scripture has said, out of his heart will flow rivers of living water. But this He spoke concerning the Spirit, whom those believing in Him would receive; for the Holy Spirit was not yet given, because Jesus was not yet glorified." This relationship between the Spirit of God and Christians was entirely new. It happened at Pentecost when the promised Spirit was sent in fulfilment of Christ's words in John 14:17.

In John 14:18 you can sense the love of Christ when He says, "I will not leave you orphans; I will come to you." Orphans are very dear to God's heart. God made provision for the special care of widows and orphans, in both the Old and New Testaments. Orphans suggest those who, for whatever reason, were abandoned. It is incredibly touching to know that Jesus, who was about to be abandoned at the Cross when He sacrificed Himself for our sins, promises never to abandon us: "I will come to you." By this He meant that, through the indwelling Spirit of God, Christ would always be with us. We are assured of the Lord: "I will never leave you nor forsake you."

Day 10

Tuesday

The Holy Spirit: Another teacher

But the Helper, the Holy Spirit, whom the Father will send in My name, He will teach you all things, and bring to your remembrance all things that I said to you. (John 14:26)

I am looking at my hands as I type. My brain is telling my hands what to do. But my hands would never know what my brain wants them to do unless they were connected to it by my nervous system. So it is with the Christian. We know the presence and power of Christ through the indwelling Spirit of God, who links us to Him in heaven.

In John 14:25-26 we learn it is the Father who would send the Spirit in the name of Christ. The Holy Spirit would be sent when Christ's work was finished and He was glorified in heaven. Jesus Himself had taught His disciples whilst He was with them. They did not always take notice or remember or understand His teaching. The Lord says that the Holy Spirit would "bring to your remembrance all things that I said to you." The Spirit would recall to the apostles' memory all Christ's words, and through this means the Scriptures were completed. But the Spirit would also teach them "all things". What was not always understood and obeyed when Christ was on earth would be able to be understood and obeyed through the indwelling Spirit of God. He is our great Teacher now, as Christ had been to His disciples when He was on earth. It is the indwelling Spirit of God who enables us to understand the word of God and to fulfil God's will in our lives.

John 15 is about fruit-bearing. Jesus describes Himself as the true vine, and we are described as branches through which His life is seen in the fruit we bear. In verse 8 He says, "By this My father is glorified, that you bear much fruit; so you will be My disciples." The indwelling Spirit of God demonstrates we are Christ's disciples by producing the fruit of the Spirit in our lives. This brings glory to God the Father. The fruit of the Spirit is described in Galatians 5:22-26. There is *one* fruit, which has many characteristics, such as love, joy and peace.

In the last two verses of chapter 15 the Lord Jesus speaks of the Spirit of God as the Helper, and the Spirit of truth. Christ was full of grace and truth, and so the Spirit is characterised by grace, as the Helper, and truth, because He is the Spirit of truth. In chapter 14 the Lord Jesus described the ministry of the Holy Spirit in relation to the past. In 15:26-27 Jesus explains the Spirit's ministry in terms of the present: "He will testify of Me." The work of the Spirit is Christ-centred. He witnesses to the Person and work of Christ. In verse 27 Jesus looks on to the Spirit's witness in the apostles who had been with Jesus throughout His earthly ministry. Witnessing to Christ is done only in the power of the Holy Spirit. By abiding in Christ through day-by-day communion and obedience, the Spirit of God empowers us to be effective witnesses to Christ in this world. May this be our daily experience as we live in a world which is in so much need of the One who is full of grace and truth.

Day 11

Wednesday

The Holy Spirit: Another guide

When He, the Spirit of truth, has come, He will guide you into all truth. (John 16:13)

He will glorify Me. (John 16:14)

The promise of the Spirit in John 16 is in two parts. In verses 8-11, the Spirit's work in the world is outlined; then in verses 12-15 the Spirit's work amongst Christians is further explained by the Lord Jesus.

In verse 8 the Lord Jesus explained that, when the Holy Spirit came, He would "convict the world concerning sin and righteousness and judgment". This powerful work was first seen at Pentecost in Acts 2. The Spirit of God, through Peter's preaching, convicted the crowd of the sin of not believing in Christ and of crucifying Him. The Spirit then presented the righteousness of God in raising Christ from the dead and exalting Him in heaven. Finally, the Spirit of God warns of judgement and the need to be saved. These themes of sin, righteousness and judgement are used by the Spirit of God to convince people of their need for Christ. Three thousand people turned to Christ at Pentecost to form the Church of God on earth. This work of the Holy Spirit continues to this day through the witness of the people of God. The Holy Spirit's work is based entirely on Christ's finished work on the cross, His resurrection and glorification, and His defeat of Satan: "the ruler of this world is judged" (v. 11).

In chapter 14 the Lord Jesus spoke of the Holy Spirit bringing His words to their remembrance. In 16:13 Jesus mentions another aspect of the work of the Spirit: "He will tell you things to come." We have seen how the Spirit of God's ministry has a connection to the past: "He will teach you all things, and bring to your remembrance all things that I said to you." It also has a connection to the present: "He will testify of Me" and "He will guide you into all truth". And it has a link to the future: "He will tell you things to come."

The word of God is the great witness to the promise of the Saviour, His earthly and heavenly ministry and the revelation of "things to come". Through the Scriptures, the Holy Spirit continuously presents Jesus Christ to our hearts as the One who "is the same yesterday, today, and forever" (Hebrews 13:8).

Zermatt in Switzerland is a beautiful Alpine town that lies beneath the majestic Matterhorn, one of the most distinctive mountains in the world. In the town there used to live an old guide who lived well into his nineties. He spent all his life leading visitors up to the summit of the Matterhorn. He had made the ascent more times than anyone else and never tired of the journey. This remarkable old man reminded me of the Holy Spirit, who, just like the Saviour, came down to earth to minister the glory of Christ to our hearts and to guide us into the truth of God on that upward journey into heaven. He never tires of this journey. Jesus was sent by the Father into the world as the Saviour. So the Holy Spirit is sent by the Father and Son, as our Helper, Teacher and Guide.

Day 12

Thursday

The Holy Spirit: Another Blesser

"Fellowship of the Spirit."   *(Philippians 2:1)*

"All Scripture", Paul reminds Timothy in 2 Timothy 3:16, is "God-breathed" (NIV), that is, of the Spirit. Peter confirms this in 2 Peter 1:21: "Prophecy never came by the will of man, but holy men of God spoke as they were moved by the Holy Spirit."

I was reminded recently in rereading Luke 15 of the involvement of the whole of the Trinity in our salvation. The Lord Jesus, as the Shepherd, finds the lost sheep. The Holy Spirit, like the woman, searches to find the lost coin, just like the Spirit searches tirelessly to lead people to Christ. Finally the father receives his lost son back into his house. The son was convicted of his sin and was led to repentance. The Spirit's work of conviction leads us to Christ. When the father received his son back again we have some remarkable illustrations of the ministry and blessings of the Holy Spirit:

In love, the father received his son. The Spirit leads us to the knowledge of the Father: "You [have] received the Spirit of adoption by whom we cry out, 'Abba, Father.' The Spirit Himself bears witness with our spirit that we are the children of God" (Romans 8:15-16).

The son had the best robe put on him. The Spirit brings us into the good of knowing that we stand before God clothed in Christ's righteousness: "not by works of righteousness which we have done, but according to His mercy He saved us, through the washing of regeneration and renewing of the Holy Spirit, whom He poured out on us abundantly through Jesus Christ our Saviour" (Titus 3:5-6).

The son was given a ring, the symbol of authority and power. We have the Spirit's indwelling power: "Greater is He who is in you than he who is in the world" (1 John 4:4, AV).

The son was given shoes: "Walk in the Spirit" (Galatians 5:16 and 25).

Finally, the fatted calf was killed, and a great family meal was enjoyed in a time of family fellowship and joy: the "fellowship of the Spirit" (Philippians 2:1).

God is the most generous giver. He has given us His Son for our salvation, and He has given us His Spirit to become worshippers and witnesses. May we ensure that we do not grieve this Holy Person: "And do not grieve the Holy Spirit of God, by whom you were sealed for the day of redemption" (Ephesians 4:30). We also have to ensure His work is not "quenched" by our disobedience: "Do not quench the Spirit" (1 Thessalonians 5:19).

In 1 Corinthians 6:19-20 we are reminded that our bodies are the temples of the Holy Spirit: "Do you not know that your body is the temple of the Holy Spirit who is in you, whom you have from God, and you are not your own? For you are bought at a price; therefore glorify God in your body and in your spirit which are God's." When Jesus visited the temple at Jerusalem, it had become a den of thieves and robbers. As He cleared the temple in John 2, He said, "Take these things away! Do not make My Father's house a house of merchandise" (v. 16). The Spirit of God indwells our hearts. We are to ensure our hearts are not cluttered by things which should not be there and which hinder the Holy Spirit's power and blessing in our lives. "The God of peace Himself sanctify you completely; and may your whole spirit, soul, and body be preserved blameless at the coming of our Lord Jesus Christ" (1 Thessalonians 5:23).

Day 13

Friday

A jar of oil and a hand full of arrows

When the vessels were full, she said to her son, "Bring me another vessel." *(2 Kings 4:6)*

And the man of God was angry with him, and said, "You should have struck five or six times." *(2 Kings 13:19)*

It may not seem obvious, but these two scriptures teach us a lot about faith. In the first incident, a widow came to Elisha because her husband had died. She was in debt and to pay the debt her two sons were going to be taken into slavery. Elisha asked what she had in the house. All she had was a jar of oil. Elisha told her to collect as many empty vessels as she could, then to shut herself in her house with her sons. Finally, she had to pour the jar of oil into all the vessels. She obeyed his instructions completely, and every vessel was filled. Elisha told her to sell the oil, pay her debt and use the remaining money to support her and her children.

At the end of Elisha's life, it wasn't a poor widow who came to see him but Joash, the king of Israel. Joash respected Elisha and wept for the prophet, crying, "O my father, my father, the chariots of Israel and their horsemen!" These were virtually the same words Elisha cried out when Elijah was taken from him into heaven by a whirlwind (2 Kings 2:12). They marked both the beginning and the end of Elisha's ministry of faith. Elisha wanted the king to have the same faith. His last act was to ask the king to take a bow, shoot an arrow through a window and strike the remaining arrows on the ground. This all symbolised the victory God wanted the king to have over his Syrian enemies. But he only struck the ground three times. Elisha was angry with the king and said, "You should have struck five or six times; then you would have struck Syria till you had destroyed it! But now you will strike Syria only three times."

There is a stark contrast between the widow and the king. The widow came in all her need to the only man who could save her. Elisha told her what to do, she acted in complete obedience, and her family was saved and blessed. Joash was a king. He loved and looked up to the great prophet. But he did not understand that the prophet wanted to bring him into the victory of faith. Elisha does everything to demonstrate that God wanted to bless the king, and guided him to act in faith. But Joash half-heartedly strikes the ground just three times. The widow did not run out of faith, but out of vessels to display it. The king ran out of faith.

We can have every support in our Christian lives and lean heavily upon others. I thank God for every spiritual brother and sister who has supported me in my pathway of faith. They encouraged me to have faith in God, to really trust Him and not to think that my smallness was an obstacle to God's greatness: rather, to remember the words of Asa, king of Judah, "Lord, it is nothing for You to help, whether with many or with those who have no power; help us, O Lord our God, for we rest on You, and in Your name we go against this multitude. O Lord, You are our God; do not let man prevail against You!" (2 Chronicles 14:11).

"Simple faith honours God and God honours simple faith" (Mary Winslow, 1774–1854).

Day 14

Saturday

The silent power of a worthy walk

I, therefore, the prisoner of the Lord, beseech you to walk worthy of the calling with which you were called, with all lowliness and gentleness, with longsuffering, bearing with one another in love.
(Ephesians 4:1-2)

I remember being present at the birth of my daughter Anna and being overwhelmed by the tiny bundle of life I held gently in my arms. I was also amazed at the speed of her development. There was an experiment in which Olympic-standard athletes were asked to imitate the movements of a tiny child. The scientists discovered that mature adults could not continue the repetitive motions of a baby for the same length of time. Our natural lives begin with an explosion of energy and development. Paul always looked for spiritual progress in himself and his fellow Christians. This progress is seen in the way a Christian lives. And Ephesians 4 begins with the Christian's walk.

The first three chapters of Paul's letter to the Ephesians are devoted to God's will, work and wisdom manifested in the Church of Christ. Chapters 4 to 6 are concerned about the practical implications of that teaching in the life of Christians. This is not limited to our personal responsibilities, but includes how we act in fellowship together.

In verse 1, Paul appeals to the Christians at Ephesus to "walk worthy of the calling with which you were called". It is a call to live in a way which honours the One who had called them. In 2 Timothy 2:4 we have a similar example. Paul writes about the soldier's commitment to please the one who enlisted him.

Also, in 1 Corinthians 6:20 we read, "For you are bought with a price: therefore glorify God in your body, and in your spirit, which are God's." This consistency between our calling and conduct is vital. If we do not live lives which are consistent with our faith, then our Christian testimony fails. The extent to which we appreciate how much God has done for us will determine how well we live for Him.

In verse 2, Paul outlines some of the things which should characterise us in this walk: humility, gentleness, patience, and bearing with one another. These are features that may seem disadvantages in an aggressive world. But we see them so clearly in the life of the most powerful man who ever lived on earth, Jesus Christ. Meekness is not weakness; it is the quietness of power.

The first time I ever sat in an electric car it seemed like any other car until we set off. It moved slowly and quietly, and then accelerated quickly and powerfully, but even then in quietness. In John 1 Andrew and his fellow disciple saw Jesus "as He walked"; they followed Him, and He invited them to "abide" or "to stay" with Him. That changed their lives. John later writes, "He who says he abides in Him ought himself also to walk just as He walked." God has given us eternal life through the Lord Jesus, who died for us and now lives for us. The Spirit of God indwells our hearts, and the word of God is in our possession. We have everything we need to enable us to live like our Saviour. We live in a noisy world. May we walk through it in the quiet, powerful witness of grace.

Day 15

Sunday

Walking in worship

"So you shall tell my father of all my glory in Egypt, and of all that you have seen." *(Genesis 45:13)*

"Do not quarrel on the way." *(Genesis 45:24, ESV)*

Joseph was loved by his father, Jacob. But he was hated by his brothers. They cast him into a pit and sold him into slavery, and Joseph suffered injustice and imprisonment. In all this suffering, he was faithful to God, and God was with him. God took him out of prison to become the saviour of the great nation of Egypt and to save his own family. God was foretelling, at the start of the Bible, a coming Saviour, His Son Jesus Christ. The Lord Jesus came to His people Israel. Rejected by them, betrayed by Judas for money, Jesus was handed over to the Roman rulers to be crucified. Joseph came out of prison, a picture of resurrection, to become a saviour. Jesus defeated death and is the Saviour of the world. Egypt bowed the knee to Joseph. God has promised that every knee shall bow and every tongue shall confess that Jesus Christ is Lord to the glory of God the Father (see Philippians 2:10-11).

At the end of Genesis 44 Joseph's brothers were in fear of judgement from Joseph, the lord of Egypt. But at the start of Genesis 45 Joseph declares, "I am Joseph. Is my father still alive?" (v. 3, ESV). Then he says those beautiful words "Please come near to me" (v. 4). This scene overflows with the love Joseph had for his father and his brothers. And it gives our hearts a remarkable impression of the wonder of the love of Christ.

Joseph sends his brothers back home to bring Jacob to Egypt with the words, "So you shall tell my father of all my glory in Egypt, and of all that you have seen." This morning, as we remember the Lord Jesus, we can sense the Lord saying to us, in the words "Remember Me" – "Please come near to Me." And we have a fresh opportunity to speak to the God and Father of our Saviour, the Lord Jesus Christ. We contemplate His glorious Person and the depth of His love in saving us.

Have you ever thought about what Joseph's brothers told their father Jacob? Each one would have their own experiences of being in Joseph's presence and realising what he had done for them and the majesty in which he stood. They would combine their impressions and bring joy to the heart of their father. Once, God opened the heavens to declare, "This is my beloved Son, in whom I am well pleased" (Matthew 3:17). Now we, God's children, speak to our Father in heaven of the Person who fills His heart and ours.

But Joseph also said to his brothers, "Do not quarrel along the way." Worship can soon be forgotten as the pressures of life put our relationships under stress. It is essential to the Lord that the oneness we express in worship is also expressed in our daily lives. We read powerful Scriptures, sing beautiful words, and speak Spirit-given thoughts as we remember the Lord. This is not to last for a brief hour, but it should shape our lives and make us tender-hearted, loving one another and showing to the world that we are one in Christ Jesus.

Day 16

Monday

Unity of the Spirit

Endeavouring to keep the unity of the Spirit in the bond of peace.
(Ephesians 4:3)

The unity of the Spirit is the oneness of the members of the body of Christ. It is established by the Holy Spirit. Christ is the head of the church, and every true believer is a member of the body of Christ. We must not confuse uniformity with unity; neither should the rich diversity of members be thought of as disunity.

In Exodus 26 the building of the Tabernacle is described. The walls of the Tabernacle were made of wooden boards overlaid with gold. Each board stood on two silver sockets and had four rings. Through these rings ran four external poles. The purpose was to connect the boards together. A fifth bar ran through the centre of the boards. This construction is a striking illustration of the Spirit of God establishing and keeping unity. The four external poles illustrate our responsibility to act to keep, in a practical sense, the unity which the Spirit has produced. The four features of Christ – lowliness, gentleness, longsuffering and bearing with one another in love – are essential to maintaining the unity of the Spirit. These features of Christ are part of the fruit of the Spirit (Galatians 5:22-23), needed to maintain the unity of the Spirit.

We do this "in the bond of peace" (v. 3). The Lord Jesus "kept" those disciples the Father had given Him (John 17:12). He is the Good Shepherd. To avoid disunity we need the Shepherd's wisdom to express the "bond of peace". James describes this wisdom as being from above and "pure, then peaceable, gentle, willing to yield, full of mercy and good fruits, without partiality and without hypocrisy" (James 3:17).

In verses 4-6 Paul outlines three relationships which we can think of as three circles. First, there is one body of Christ and one Holy Spirit (v. 4), linked to one calling and one hope. The calling refers to God calling us to salvation and all its blessings. The Ephesians had been without hope and without God (2:12). Then they were called and accepted in Christ (Ephesians 1:6), and possessed the "blessed hope" (Titus 2:13). This first circle includes all true believers who are members of the body of Christ and indwelt by the Spirit of God.

Then there is one Lord, the Lord Jesus Christ; one faith in Christ, and one baptism. This second circle is people's relationship to the Lord Jesus and includes all true believers, but also professing Christians. It is not enough, however, to be baptised and outwardly profess Christ as Lord. Many people are attached to the Christian faith and have been baptised. But they have never received Him as Saviour and don't have life in Christ. The last circle is the relationship to the one God and Father of all. God is described as being above all. God is recognised by many people, both within and outside of Christendom.

The Christian knows God in the reality of His person and His power in creation. The Christian has faith in the Lord Jesus Christ and witnesses to a new life in Christ. The Christian is indwelt by the Holy Spirit, is a member of the body of Christ having been called by God, and has the hope of one day being with and like Christ forever. How important it is to express the love of Christ through our unity.

Day 17

Tuesday

The gifts to the Church

And He Himself gave some to be apostles, some prophets, some evangelists, and some pastors and teachers. *(Ephesians 4:11)*

In verse 7 Paul explains that every Christian has a gift given by Christ. It is essential to see that a gift is just that: something which is given. The gifts are for the benefit of all the people of God. They should be used with humility and in dependence upon the One who gives them. Paul quotes Psalm 68:18 in verse 8 to describe Christ's victorious death, His power in resurrection and His return in glory to heaven. After battles, victorious kings gave gifts to their servants. Christ has given gifts to His people. These are given to equip the saints for the ministry of building up the body of Christ. There are three main passages in the New Testament which teach us about spiritual gifts. In Romans 12:3-8 the gifts are outlined in relation to the service of God. In 1 Corinthians 12 the gifts are to be used under the direction and power of the Spirit of God. Here, in Ephesians 4, the gifts are linked with the Lord Jesus building up His church, the body of Christ.

The apostles and prophets were chosen and gifted to undertake the foundational work described in Ephesians 2:19-20. The church continues to be built up from this foundation. A foundation is laid once. No one has the right to come along today claiming to be an apostle or prophet with fresh revelation. The Bible is the complete record of God's revelation and all that we need for faith and practice. And Jesus is the Alpha and the Omega (Revelation 1:8).

An evangelist is not merely a preacher, but someone gifted by God to lead people to Christ. Interestingly, there is only one man in the New Testament called an evangelist. This was "Philip the evangelist" (Acts 21:8). In Acts 8 we read about his evangelism and are given a pattern for the evangelist, one who finds people to preach to; he is proactive. There are two ways to evangelise, publicly and personally. We need gifted evangelists to do this work. The Lord Jesus encourages us to "pray the Lord of the harvest to send out labourers into His harvest" (Matthew 9:38). We should never lose sight of the importance of the evangelist. Even if we do not possess this gift we can still "do the work of an evangelist", which Paul encouraged his young friend to do in 2 Timothy 4:5.

A pastor is a shepherd who builds up and protects the flock. If a sheep gets lost, the shepherd finds it. The shepherd ensures the sheep get the right kind of food and that they are protected from danger. You can see what a powerful illustration the shepherd is of all the work involved in looking after "the flock of God". The pastor has to be self-sacrificing and an example to the Lord's people (1 Peter 5:2-4).

The teacher communicates the word of God to the people of God under the direction of the Holy Spirit. The effect is that the listeners grow in their own understanding of, and obedience to, the truth. A teacher is expected to demonstrate the reality of what he teaches in his own life. He a person who never stops learning from the Lord Jesus, who is our Apostle, Prophet, Evangelist, Shepherd and Teacher.

Day 18

Wednesday

The building up of the Body

For the equipping of the saints for the work of ministry, for the edifying of the body of Christ.   (Ephesians 4:12)

Paul teaches that the use of gifts builds up all believers, and so the church grows. There are several features to this growth. And In verse 13 we have the knowledge of the Son of God. This is not a sterile, intellectual knowledge but a living, deepening knowledge of the Lord which changes His people – us – into His likeness.

This also leads to maturity. God created Adam and Eve as adults, not children. Childhood can be wonderful, and there are many lessons in its experience. But God looks for growth and maturity. In verse 14 Paul uses children as a picture of instability. He compares the effects of false doctrine upon the immature Christian to a rudderless ship, tossed one way, then the other by winds. In verse 15 he explains it is the truth of the word of God (John 17:17) that keeps us from such dangers and ensures our spiritual growth. The truth of God's word is to be communicated in love to encourage and build each other up in our Christian faith. Truth can be spoken without love, but this can drive away those we want to help. Love does not change the truth but presents it in the most appealing way, and so we grow to be like Christ. It is always heart-warming for parents to hear that others see them in their children. It is God's desire to see the characteristics of the Lord Jesus in us.

Christ is the head of the body. Paul again uses the human body to make his point. Christ is lived out in our lives by the power and direction of the Holy Spirit. We fulfil our different roles in the body by using the gift Christ has given us. In this way, not only do we grow individually but the whole church benefits. It grows and is built up in love: "The whole body, joined and knit together by what every joint supplies, according to the effective working by which every part does its share, causes growth of the body for the edifying of itself in love" (Ephesians 4:16).

It is not merely growing but being built up. There are two aspects to natural growth, food and fitness. It is the same spiritually: we can receive a lot of ministry of God's word both individually and as the people of God. And we can become used to just listening. But listening to God's word is just the beginning. We need to believe it in our hearts, meditate upon it in our minds and live it out day by day. It exercises our faith and teaches us God's faithfulness. It makes us stronger and blesses and protects us spiritually and morally. We should share our experience of God's word and His revelation to our hearts with one another. In this way, we grow together as the people of God and are enabled to share, defend and contend for the faith.

The simple practice of reading, marking and learning from the word of God is a very helpful one. First, we read the Bible; then we prayerfully consider what we have read and what God is teaching us. Then, with worshipping hearts, we follow His commands, trust His promises, enjoy His blessings, express His love, and communicate our faith.

Day 19

Thursday

The power of a broken heart

Reproach has broken my heart. (Psalm 69:20)

He has sent Me to heal the brokenhearted. (Luke 4:18)

Pilate brought the Lord Jesus out before the representatives of the nation of Israel on two occasions. He announced Jesus first with the words, "Behold the man!" and later with the words "Behold your king!" (John 19:5 and 14). We were not there to see the Lord so shamefully and cruelly treated and paraded with a crown thorns and robes of mockery. But, by faith, we have an understanding that it was then that the Lord went through the experience of reproach breaking His heart. He heard so clearly the chants expressed in a harmony of hatred, "Away with Him, away with Him! Crucify Him!" (John 19:15).

In John 12, Mary broke a box of precious and expensive spikenard and poured the contents on to the feet of Jesus and the house was filled with its fragrance. Christ's broken-heartedness filled Calvary with the fragrance of forgiveness for enemies, love for the family, peace for the sinner, sacrifice for the world, poverty to make rich, victory in substitution and the power of a life laid down in love.

When the Lord Jesus began His work, He visited Nazareth, where He had been brought up. He announced His ministry, which would demonstrate His power as the Messiah King, the Servant of God, Son of Man and Son of God. Jesus would meet every need and never be confounded by the sorrow and sin He encountered in a needy world. In introducing this ministry,

He did not speak first about healing deafness, blindness or lameness. He talked about healing the broken-hearted.

In Exodus 3 God said to Moses, "I have surely seen the oppression of My people who are in Egypt, and have heard their cry because of their taskmasters, for I know their sorrows. So I have come down to deliver them" (vv. 7-8). He was speaking about coming down in the power of judgment to deliver a nation from slavery. He came down to "bring them up from that land to a good and large land, to a land flowing with milk and honey" (v. 8).

At Calvary we see God coming down in the power of His love for the salvation of the world. This love was demonstrated by Christ being oppressed and knowing the sorrow of a broken heart. The suffering of Christ has saved us. And the One whose heart was broken has still the power to heal the broken-hearted. His love continues to reach out to a broken world. And it also reaches out to so many of the people of God who experience broken hearts. The reasons for this experience are manifold. It can be because of personal failure, dashed hopes, loneliness, rejection, family issues, divorce, ill-health and bereavement. These things can overwhelm us. It is difficult to see a broken heart, but the Lord sees. He has the power to come down in the sympathy of His grace to take us out of despair and to lift us up. In doing so, He transforms the broken-hearted into the tender-hearted (Ephesians 4:32).

Day 20

Friday

The resolute heart

But Daniel purposed in his heart. (Daniel 1:8)

The opening verses of the book of Daniel do not make good reading. They describe disaster, defeat, destruction and sophisticated slavery. The northern kingdom of Israel had already been enslaved by the Assyrians. Now Judah was overwhelmed by Nebuchadnezzar, king of Babylon. The brightest young people were transported to Babylon to be absorbed into its culture and introduced to its gods in what was the darkest day in the descent of God's people. God had taken the Children of Israel out of slavery in Egypt to "bring them up from that land to a good and large land, to a land flowing with milk and honey" (Exodus 3:8). Now, they returned to slavery – in Babylon. This was different slavery. It was not the bitterness of being controlled by cruel and unreasonable taskmasters in Egypt. No, Babylon was more dangerous. It warmly embraced the people of God with its riches, wickedness, power and opportunity. It is the very opposite of the embrace of the father in Luke 15.

Then we have one of God's great interventions, "But Daniel". It is extraordinary how, often against a background of danger and disaster, God intervenes in the heart of just one person. He worked in the hearts of men and women like Abraham, Moses, Gideon, Ruth, Hannah, Samuel. And he also worked in the hearts of Daniel, Ezra, Esther and Nehemiah. These saints of God had resolute hearts and clear-thinking, spiritual minds. They believed God in the face of incredible odds. In situations where the power of Satan, either as a roaring lion or an angel of light, was so evident, they were victorious by faith. They were as wise as serpents and as harmless as doves. These men and women proved to us the power of faith and the reality of God's presence. Alongside them were many, many nameless people of faith who, like the 7000 in Israel (1 Kings 19:18), were known only to God.

Daniel started by addressing his diet. He was determined to live in personal devotion to God, no matter what choices others made. He was wise in how he approached the case, but there was no doubt it was a line he would not cross. Our personal devotion to Christ is central to our pathway of faith. And we have to be careful about what we choose to introduce into our hearts and minds. We live in a world that is continually trying to influence, persuade, and shape our lives without reference to the God we believe in. It will warmly embrace us in unbelief, but not in faith. Daniel is a beautiful Old Testament example of the New Testament teaching, "Do not be conformed to this world, but be transformed by the renewing of your mind, that you may prove what is that good and acceptable and perfect will of God" (Romans 12:2).

God has a pathway for each one of His children. We need a resolute heart of faith in the Lord Jesus for Him to take us along that pathway and to prove in our lives His presence and perfect will.

And like Daniel, we have our Shadrachs, Meshachs and Abed-Negos encouraging us along the way.

Day 21

Saturday

The transformed heart

Do not be conformed to this world, but be transformed by the renewing of your mind, that you may prove what is that good and acceptable and perfect will of God. (Romans 12:2)

At the beginning of Romans 12 Paul appeals to his fellow Christians, by the mercies of God communicated through His love, to present their bodies as living sacrifices. This is the spiritually intelligent and holy response of our lives to God.

We are not to be conformed to this world (v. 2). "Conformed" means to be shaped into something different. It is rather like a jelly mould emphasising a visible change. Instead, we are to be transformed (metamorphosis), which describes a complete transformation by God's power. The emphasis is on an inward change expressed through the character and life of a Christian. Paul encourages his readers to behave with humility and to understand and appreciate the different members of Christ's body. He outlines some of the spiritual gifts given for the building up of the church, and he describes how these should be used in spiritual ways (vv. 6-8).

Paul completes the chapter with the characteristics that demonstrate the transforming power of God's love in our hearts, minds and lives:

v. 9: a genuine love – "Let love be without hypocrisy."

v. 10: a compassionate and considerate love – "Be kindly affectionate to one another with brotherly love, in honour giving preference to one another."

v. 11: a hardworking love – "Not lagging in diligence, fervent in spirit, serving the Lord."

v. 12: a rejoicing, patient and prayerful love – "Rejoicing in hope, patient in tribulation, continuing steadfastly in prayer."

v. 13: a love that gives – "Distributing to the needs of the saints, given to hospitality."

v. 14: a love that blesses – "Bless those who persecute you; bless and do not curse."

v. 15: a love that sympathises – "Rejoice with those who rejoice, and weep with those who weep."

v. 16: a unifying and lowly love – "Be of the same mind toward one another, do not set your mind on high things, but associate with the humble. Do not be wise in your own opinion."

v. 17: a love that suffers evil but does good – "Repay no one evil for evil, have regard for good things in the sight of all men."

v. 18: a peaceable love – "If it is possible, as much as depends on you, live peaceably with all men."

v. 19-21: a love that overcomes – "Do not be overcome by evil, but overcome evil with good."

This is the love of God, which has been poured into our hearts by the Holy Spirit (see Romans 5:5).

Day 22

Sunday

The Lamb that was slain

Then Mary took a pound of very costly oil of spikenard, anointed the feet of Jesus, and wiped His feet with her hair. And the house was filled with the fragrance of the oil. (John 12:3)

Then I looked, and I heard the voice of many angels around the throne, the living creatures, and the elders; and the number of them was ten thousand times ten thousand, and thousands of thousands, saying with a loud voice: "Worthy is the Lamb who was slain" (Revelation 5:11-12).

Mary was heavily criticised for breaking a box of precious spikenard on the Lord's feet. But it was the response of worship to the One who is the "Resurrection and the Life". She alone discerned the pathway the Lord was taking to lay down His life at Calvary and to be buried (v. 7). It was from the grave that the God of peace "brought up our Lord Jesus from the dead, that great Shepherd of the sheep" (Hebrews 13:20). But, the Lord Jesus does not speak in verse 7 of His resurrection. He speaks about how much He valued worship from the hearts of His own people, who would never forget that He went into death for them.

Mary did not speak, but in Revelation 5, the redeemed company and the angelic host gather together and with one voice respond in worship to the Lamb that was slain. We glory in the resurrection and ascension of our Lord Jesus. We joy in the words of the hymn that "sorrow's night is o'er", but neither time nor eternity will erase the memory of the love that took the Lord Jesus into death. It touched His heart that Mary appreciated the extent of His love. The day is coming when the redeemed people of God and hosts of heaven will together express that appreciation and be overwhelmed by His worthiness.

Angels share in the worship. They were witnesses to His eternal glory and they followed Him and served Him in amazement during His lowly life on earth. They could not minister to Him at the cross, but they gloried in His resurrection and ascension in glory. We, not angels, are the recipients of the love which took the Lord of life into death. Our names are engraved upon the palms of His hands, and we are in His heart. Each one of us is a trophy and story of grace, and we each have an opportunity to follow the Saviour who so loved us. The thief on the cross had the briefest of time to respond to Jesus Christ. But what a glorious response it was and, like Mary, what joy it brought to the Saviour's heart amidst the horror of Calvary. I am sure this dying thief would have wished he could have spent his life responding to the Saviour who he discovered loved him. Instead, he stands as a witness to the fact that every single one of us is brought into life by simple faith in the Son of God "who loved me and gave Himself for me". His love alone takes us to glory.

This morning may our hearts be filled with holy worship as we bow afresh at the feet of the One in whose heart we were as He died upon the tree. The One who is now the centre of heaven.

Day 23

Monday

Samuel and Eli

*And the child Samuel grew in stature, and in favour both with the L*ORD *and men.* (1 Samuel 2:26)

Samuel's life is told within the context of five relationships: His relationships with his mother Hannah, Eli the High Priest, the nation of Israel, Saul the first king of Israel, and David, Israel's shepherd king. But above all was his relationship with God. Hannah laid the foundation of Samuel's life. She has left us some important practical lessons about the ministry of a godly mother. This ministry was rooted in the responsibility to pray for our children before they are even born and throughout the rest of their lives. She was a worshipper of God who was willing to sacrifice for her child, and she created a home that became the centre of Samuel's great ministry. This was the mother Samuel had, and her commitment to him prepared Samuel for a life of service for God.

But Samuel's relationship with Eli was of a different kind. When we first meet Eli, he mistakes Hannah's spiritual behaviour for drunkenness. We soon discover that God held him responsible for the appalling behaviour of his sons, who held high positions as priests. In her obedience to God, it seemed Hannah had given her son into the hands of a man who lacked spiritual leadership and tolerated gross immorality in his own family. God held Eli responsible for the spiritual corruption at the heart of Israel's decline. But Hannah had not given her son to Eli, but to the God who had given Samuel to her. Hannah's faith was in God, and God began to work in Samuel's heart in the midst the darkness of Eli's house.

Despite being in such a problematic situation, Samuel grew in favour with God and men, a statement reminiscent of the Lord Jesus in Luke 2:40 and 52. In 1 Samuel 3:1, we learn that things were at such a spiritual low in Israel that God's word was rare. When God's word does come, it is to Samuel when he is still a boy. On the one hand, this is very condemning, because there was no adult that God could use. On the other hand, it demonstrates that God was working in a new and fresh way. Samuel did not know God, nor had the word of God been revealed to him (3:7). And as God speaks to him, Samuel mistakes it for Eli calling him. The old man eventually realises that God was speaking to the boy and gives him some wise advice: "Speak, Lord, for Your servant hears." This attitude marked Samuel for the rest of his life. What God said, he did. When we discover the same childlike ability to listen and to do what God asks us, we experience His presence and power.

God's message to Samuel was not a happy one. It foretold the judgement of Eli's house. When Eli asks Samuel what God had said, the boy is not marked by pride that God had spoken to him above all others, but with a sadness that He spoke in judgement. Like the Lord Jesus, Samuel's ministry was characterised by grace and truth.

Following this meeting with God, we learn that "Samuel grew, and the Lord was with him" (3:19), he was "established as a prophet" (v. 20) and "the Lord revealed Himself to Samuel" (v. 21). To be a useful servant of God, we have to be prepared by and learn from the Lord directly. It is no good living our lives off other Christians' experiences. God's word has to have a direct effect in our hearts so we can fulfil His purposes and witness to His reality, no matter how dark the day.

Day 24

Tuesday

Samuel and Israel

And the word of Samuel came to all Israel.   *(1 Samuel 4:1)*

Samuel's relationship with the nation of Israel begins at today's verse. Just when we think things cannot get worse, something more dreadful happens. 1 Samuel 4 begins with Samuel's introduction to the nation he was to serve for such a long time. It ends with the birth of Ichabod, which means "The glory has departed from Israel." The conflict between Israel and the Philistines, which is recorded in this chapter, culminates in Eli's sons, Hophni and Phinehas, bringing the Ark of the Covenant into battle at the demand of the elders of Israel. God will not bless a disobedient nation. They expected a victory like the defeat of Jericho, when the ark was a focus of blessing, but they were tragically mistaken. Israel was defeated, Hophni and Phinehas were killed, the ark was taken, and the shock of the news caused the death of Eli and the birth of Ichabod. These awful events solemnly remind us of the folly of pretending to serve God outwardly when in our hearts and by our practice we are so far from Him – what has been described as "high talk and low walk". Samuel's life teaches us the vital truth that God looks on the heart.

In our hypocrisy, we can fool strangers, friends, even family and, above all, ourselves. But we can never fool God. The hypocrisy of the Israelites is a warning to us. Israel had not stopped worshipping God and in their distress they prayed to Him. But they also continued to worship idols. It is possible, and often at the root of our own spiritual weakness, for us to worship as Christians but have things in our lives which are effectively idols. It is surprising how we can devote immense amounts of time, energy and resources to transient things like sport, entertainment, money and material possessions, to the extent that the Lord takes second or even a lower place in our lives. This is why the apostle John's warning, "Little children, keep yourselves from idols" is so important.

The Ark's return to Israel in chapter 6 is a wonderful story, which led Israel back to God. Samuel led their return. He tells them, "If you return to the LORD with all your hearts, then put away the foreign gods and the Ashtoreths from among you, and prepare your hearts for the LORD, and serve Him only; and He will deliver you" (1 Samuel 7:3). Israel listened to Samuel and forsook the idols which they had worshipped.

Samuel was a man of prayer. He brought Israel together with the promise, "Gather all Israel to Mizpah, and I will pray to the LORD for you" (7:5). In verse 8 the people asked Samuel not to cease to pray for them and in verse 9 Samuel cries to the Lord and the Lord answers. Victory over the Philistines follows and afterwards Samuel erects a stone and calls it "Ebenezer" – "Thus far the LORD has helped us." Reflecting on what God has done for us and what He wants to do in us and through us brings us to the Throne of Grace in a ministry of prayer and intercession: "I exhort first of all that supplications, prayers, intercessions, and giving of thanks be made for all men" (1 Timothy 2:1).

Day 25

Wednesday

Samuel and rejection

They have not rejected you, but they have rejected Me, that I should not reign over them. *(1 Samuel 8:7)*

Samuel served God all the days of his life. His base was his home at Ramah. There he built an altar, and it was the place to which he always returned (1 Samuel 7:17). We cannot have an effective ministry to others unless we have a strong spiritual base ourselves, a Christ-centred home. From his home, Samuel served the nation, travelling in a circuit to Bethel, Gilgal and Mizpah.

Bethel was the house of God where Jacob first received the promises of grace and set up the stone, which had been his pillow, to mark the place. There was nothing in Jacob's life which commended him to God, but God loved him. Bethel reminds us that all our blessings are through the love and grace of God (Genesis 28:13-15). At Gilgal twelve stones were erected as a memorial of the children of Israel being taken over the Jordan into the Promised Land. God had miraculously taken His people out of Egypt, and He brought them miraculously into the land. It was at Gilgal that the Israelites were circumcised and separated to God as a holy people. It was where they held the Passover and ate the old corn of the land, after which the manna ceased (Joshua 4-5). Mizpah means "watchtower". Jacob set up a pillar to mark the covenant between him and Laban (Genesis 31:45-50) as Jacob returned home as God promised he would. It was to Mizpah that Samuel brought Israel and called upon them to return to God and where God blessed them. There Samuel erected the stone called Ebenezer to remind the people of God's help (1 Samuel 7:12). Bethel. Gilgal and Mizpah were constant reminders of God's love and grace, His power and holiness and His help and faithfulness. These themes marked the ministry of Samuel.

Samuel served God from childhood in a nation which was so spiritually weak. God used Samuel to revive and encourage His people. In this service for God, he suffered severe disappointments. Samuel's own children failed to follow in his footsteps and became dishonest. It is remarkable that God judged Eli for the failure of his children but never judged Samuel, although his children dishonoured God. He will hold us responsible for how we bring up our children, but ultimately, they are accountable for their own behaviour. This experience is connected to Samuel's bitter disappointment when Israel asked for a king. He learnt, through the sorrow in his own heart over his children, the sadness that was in God's heart when He told His old servant, "They (the people of God) have not rejected you, but they have rejected Me, that I should not reign over them."

Samuel never stopped loving and serving the people of God. He never turned his back upon them but continued to faithfully minister to all the people of God, despite the rejection he must have felt so profoundly. Samuel is a remarkable example of a life devoted to the service of God and the welfare of His people. He is an outstanding Old Testament illustration of the Lord's ministry, which began on earth and now continues for us in heaven: "He always lives to make intercession" (Hebrews 7:25).

Day 26

Thursday

Samuel and Saul

"Behold, to obey is better than sacrifice, And to heed than the fat of rams." (1 Samuel 15:22)

The failure of Samuel's children as judges led to Samuel's next disappointment: Israel's request for a king. Samuel's answer was to pray. He faithfully warns the people of God about the consequences of choosing a king and pleaded with them not to go down that route. But, having had the joy of leading the people back to God, he experienced the bitterness of having his spiritual advice ignored. God tells Samuel to give the nation a king. So begins the next pivotal relationship of Samuel's life: his relationship with Saul. This is the man who, in chapter 10, Samuel anoints as the first king of Israel. Saul is symbolic of man's view of things. At the beginning of chapter 9 Saul is described as a mighty man of power. He was more handsome than anyone else in Israel and stood head and shoulders above the rest of the people. Such an attractive man appealed to the people then as it does today. We are so often interested in the surface rather than the substance. But God intervened to give Saul other advantages. He gave him another heart and the gift of the Spirit (10:9-10). Saul was also marked by humility (10:22) and a following of faithful men "whose hearts God had touched" (10:26). Success followed. Soon Saul was established as king over God's people with the support of God's servant, Samuel.

In chapter 12 Samuel faithfully addresses the people of God in the power of a life lived serving God and His people. He demonstrates God's power in nature in verses 17-18 to show their dependence on the Lord. The people ask Samuel to pray for them. The tender heart of this old servant of God is summed up in verse 23: "Far be it from me that I should sin against the LORD in ceasing to pray for you; but I will teach you the good and the right way." The mark of a dedicated servant of God is the care he will always have for God's people, despite the failure that so often characterises them. A true shepherd never forsakes the flock.

It is touching to see Samuel's spiritual care for Saul. As Samuel had interceded for a nation, so he did for his king. Yet despite this support and the early promise, Saul's reign ends in disobedience, and God rejects him as king. This is summed up in chapter 15 in Samuel's words to Saul,

> "Has the LORD as great delight in burnt offerings and sacrifices,
> As in obeying the voice of the LORD?
> Behold, to obey is better than sacrifice,
> And to heed than the fat of rams ...
> Because you have rejected the word of the LORD,
> He also has rejected you from being king."

These words reflect the foundations of Samuel's service. His whole ministry emerged from his mother's obedience in giving him to God. His was a powerful ministry because he listened to and obeyed the word of God. He was prepared to confront a nation and a king rather than dishonour his God. His life teaches us how vital obedience is. The Lord Jesus says in John 14:15, "If you love Me, keep My commandments."

Saul never saw Samuel again, until after Samuel's death. Samuel mourned for king Saul. But God was about to open Samuel's eyes to a new king, David, "a man after My own heart, who will do all My will" (Acts 13:22). Samuel reminds us we are never too old to learn the ways and the wisdom of God and how, through Christ, He can turn our sorrow into joy.

Day 27

Friday

Samuel and David

For the LORD does not see as man sees; for man looks on the outward appearance, but the LORD looks at the heart.

(1 Samuel 16:7)

God tells Samuel at the beginning of chapter 16 to go to the house of Jesse to anoint a new king. This visit begins the final relationship in Samuel's long history of service, his relationship with the greatest Old Testament king of Israel, David. Samuel arrives and is introduced to Jesse's sons. He is impressed with the fine young men placed before him. But the old prophet learns afresh how God chooses His servants. God says to Samuel, "Do not look at his appearance or at his physical stature, because I have refused him. For the LORD does not see as man sees; for man looks on the outward appearance, but the LORD looks at the heart." Samuel, in his disappointment over Saul, looked for someone similar to replace him. And God took him right back to the roots of his existence – in his mother Hannah's heart. In chapter 1 Hannah spoke in her heart and the Lord remembered her. Many years later, the son that God gave to Hannah was an old man, full of disappointment at the failure of the people of God and of their king. Samuel was temporarily blinded to the way God works. In grace, God speaks to His servant's heart to remind him that it is into our hearts that God looks and from where He will always begin to work.

There was one more son of Jesse, David. And where was he? Keeping his father's sheep. It had always struck me that, when Saul was discovered, he was looking for his father's donkeys which, incidentally, he never found. They were found for him.

But David was absent from the line-up of Jesse's sons because he was keeping his father's sheep. The man who was to become the shepherd-king of Israel, who would defeat Goliath with a stone from his shepherd's sling, and who would write, "The LORD is my shepherd", is introduced to us as a shepherd keeping his father's sheep. On that day Samuel met a young man who would care for God's flock, just as Samuel had. And the prophet and great judge of Israel had the joy of anointing a new king, and lived to hear of David's victory over Goliath in the valley of Elah (ch. 17). Later, when David is persecuted by Saul, he goes and stays with Samuel at his house at Ramah (19:18). David unburdens his heart to the old servant of God. What did Samuel say to him? He may have told him about his own beginnings, the times God spoke to him, and about the responsibility and the disappointments involved in serving God. I am sure he would have told him how God looks into our hearts, and that blessing and victory come by faith and obedience. What we do know, is that God was later to say of David in Acts 13:22, "I have found David the son of Jesse, a man after My own heart, who will do all My will."

At the end of his long life of service, Samuel had the joy of knowing God's blessing and victory as he encouraged David in his future role. As we look at our own service, may God give us the grace to know the importance of being prepared by Him, and the determination to serve Him in the most difficult of circumstances. May He give us the strength to undertake responsibility, and the wisdom and patience to deal with the disappointments we will inevitably face. Finally, may He give us the joy of experiencing His blessing and victory as we serve our Lord and Saviour, share His love and encourage our fellow Christians.

Day 28

Saturday

The Gospel writers

And there are also many other things that Jesus did, which if they were written one by one, I suppose that even the world itself could not contain the books that would be written. Amen. (John 21:25)

The Holy Spirit of God chose not only the subjects of Scripture but the writers of Scripture. The four Gospels give four views of Christ. The first one, Matthew, presents Jesus as the Messiah King. Matthew was a tax collector, running a despised but very profitable business in a partnership with the occupying Roman authorities. As far as his fellow countrymen were concerned, he had betrayed his country for financial gain. The Lord Jesus simply says to Matthew, "Follow Me." He chose a man who was so far from God to be part of the small group of men who were eyewitnesses of His life and work in this world. The Spirit of God uses this converted tax collector to write the Gospel which presents the Messiah King of Israel, great David's greater Son.

Mark was a bright young Christian at the very centre of the early church. He became one of the first missionaries with Paul and Barnabas. But he found the mission field a hard place and returned to Jerusalem. Paul refused to take him on his second missionary journey because he felt Mark was unreliable. Barnabas took Mark to Cyprus and by means of his pastoral care helped his young relative. At the end of Paul's writings in 2 Timothy, we see John Mark restored and Paul commending him with affection as a useful servant of God. The Spirit of God uses Mark, a failed but restored servant, to write about Jesus as the Servant of God. Isn't God's grace extraordinary?

Luke is the only Gospel writer who was a Gentile. We don't know how he came to the Saviour. As a doctor, he lived in a world without a National Health Service, a world in which even the simplest of diseases could become life-threatening. He knew first-hand about human suffering and his own limited resources. There were no anaesthetics, no antibiotics. The Spirit of God uses this tender-hearted physician to introduce us to the Saviour, who could meet all the needs of a suffering world and remove all the distance between God and man. Through his words, we are brought into the presence of Jesus as the Son of Man.

John, in his Gospel, refers to himself as the disciple whom Jesus loved. He had a very close relationship with the Saviour as did his brother James, together with Peter. It is John that the Lord speaks to from the cross and asks to take care of His mother. To this faithful, devoted and caring disciple, the Spirit of God would one day say, "You write about the Son of God." John conveys the wonder and glory of Christ's deity and the wonder and glory of the Person and work of the Son of God in the world He had made.

The writings of these four very different men bear testimony to the Lord Jesus, which has continued over 2000 years. They present details of the Saviour which are still bringing salvation to the lost, and transforming lives, moving us in service and worship. They remind us, too, of the ability of the Lord, through the Holy Spirit, to write His story upon our hearts and to move us to follow the Lord like Matthew, to serve Him like Mark, to love Him like Luke and to worship Him like John.

Day 29

Sunday

The King of Glory

Who is this King of glory?
The L<small>ORD</small> *of hosts,*
He is the King of glory. Selah. *(Psalm 24:10)*

Psalm 22, 23 and 24 are psalms of glory. They have sometimes been titled: the Cross, the Crook and the Crown. Psalm 22 describes the sufferings of the Saviour: "My God, My God, why have You forsaken Me?" (v. 1). Psalm 23 brings before us the Saviour's shepherd care: "The L<small>ORD</small> is my shepherd" (v. 1). And Psalm 24 contemplates the sovereignty of the Saviour: "He is the King of glory" (v. 10).

We often think of the sufferings and glory of the Saviour. Psalm 22 prophetically speaks of what the Lord endured at Calvary. The Holy Spirit brings into the mind and heart of David words that express what the Lord of life would pass through as He gave Himself for us. The sufferings of the Lord bring before us the glory of His work of salvation and the wonder of His love. We see through the words of Psalm 22 the depth of what it meant for the Good Shepherd to lay down His life for the sheep.

In Psalm 23 we are reminded of the Great Shepherd in the glory of His resurrection. He lives for us on high. In Him we have everything we need: His person, His pastures, His paths, His presence, His provision and His purposes. This glory links with His ministry as our great High Priest, living for us, sympathising with us and sustaining us as we seek to follow Him on the path to glory.

When we think of the King of glory in Psalm 24, we think of the Great Shepherd and His appearing to reign as King of kings and Lord of lords. Then there will be no rejection or resistance to His power and glory. Every knee will bow to Him, and every tongue will confess the Lordship of Christ, to the glory of His Father and our Father. The Lord suffered outside the gates of Jerusalem. In that day, the gates will lift up their heads (vv. 7, 9) and the King of glory will come in.

These remarkable psalms reflect on the glories of the Son of God. Psalm 22 refers to a day when "All the ends of the world / Shall remember and turn to the Lord, / And all the families of the nations / Shall worship before You" (v. 27).

This morning, it is our hearts that are lifted up in remembrance and worship of our Saviour. We look back to the love of Christ in Psalm 22. We look up in faith to see our Saviour crowned with glory and honour in Psalm 23. And we look on in hope to our coming Saviour, the King of Glory, in Psalm 24.

> O Thou great all-gracious Shepherd,
> Shedding for us Thy life's blood,
> Unto shame and death delivered,
> All to bring us nigh to God!
> Now our willing hearts adore Thee,
> Now we taste Thy dying love,
> While by faith we come before Thee -
> Faith which lifts our souls above.

Day 30

Monday

Announcing the Saviour

For unto you is born this day in the city of David a Saviour, which is Christ the Lord. (Luke 2:11, AV)

Luke writes his Gospel to a friend called Theophilus, and it's as though he was writing a personal letter to us all. He introduces us to the world into which Jesus was born: a world dominated by the Roman Empire. Only Matthew and Luke write of the circumstances and events of Christ's birth. Matthew writes from a Jewish background and Luke as a Gentile. Luke gives more detail, beginning with the miraculous events surrounding John the Baptist's birth, before describing the vital truth of how Mary was chosen to be the mother of Jesus Christ. He tells us of the faith and worship which flowed from the hearts of Elizabeth and Mary. He describes the ordinary people whose lives became the focus of God's greatest intervention in the history of the world: the birth of the Saviour of the world. Luke puts into perspective the mighty world power of Rome and the authority of Caesar Augustus when he orders a census of his empire. This was not the power of a great monarch, but the power of God moving the whole world so that Mary and Joseph would be led to Bethlehem. Luke records the moment when the Person who occupied the centre of heaven was laid in a manger "because there was no room in the inn." These simple words describe to our hearts the arrival of the Lord of glory into His creation as a homeless child, hidden in the small crowded city of David.

It is in the hearts of ordinary people that Luke traces God's goodness. He alone tells us about the angels' glorious appearing to the shepherds in the fields outside Bethlehem. The world was oblivious to the birth of Jesus on that holy night, but heaven was not:

> "Glory to God in the highest,
> And on earth peace, good will toward men!"

Luke's Gospel reveals to us that, although the Lord was rejected as a homeless stranger on earth, He never ceased to occupy the attention and the thoughts of heaven. He records the opened heaven at the beginning of the Lord's life in Bethlehem and the opened heaven when Jesus returned to heaven in glory (Luke 24). He alone tells us of the welcome the Lord receives as a baby in the temple. His parents came with two turtle doves as a sacrifice. It was the smallest sacrifice, brought by those who could afford no more. It demonstrated the reality of the Lord Jesus entering into the poverty of this world. At the same time, worship poured out of the hearts of Simeon and Anna. This witnessed to the power of the Saviour held in the arms of this old servant of God (Luke 2:29-30).

Luke uniquely records the young boy Jesus staying behind in Jerusalem to confound the wisest men of the day. The "Ancient of Days" as a twelve-year-old! Luke gives us the first words of Jesus: "Why did you seek Me? Did you not know that I must be about My father's business?" He also records the last words of the Lord Jesus on the cross, "Father, into Your hands I commit My spirit" (Luke 23:46). Luke's Gospel describes the astonishing grace of the Lord Jesus. He traces the quiet pathway the Lord took from Bethlehem, Jerusalem and Nazareth until He is no longer hidden from the nation but announced as the Saviour of the world. Luke, the shepherds, Simeon, and Anna all came to Jesus and then witnessed to the Saviour in a world that did not know Him. Now we have the privilege to do the same.

Day 31

Tuesday

The voice of the Godhead

"You are My beloved Son; in You I am well pleased."   (Luke 3:22)

The early chapters of Luke's Gospel record the baptism of the Lord, His testing in the wilderness and the beginning of His wonderful ministry. We have a tendency to look at these events in isolation. I think it is vital to see the links between these critical moments in the life of the Lord Jesus, and to hear the voice of the Godhead.

The first voice we hear is the voice of God the Father, "You are My beloved Son; in You I am well pleased." God the Father opens the heavens at the commencement of the Lord's public ministry to declare the deity of the Lord Jesus as the Son of God and the joy He has in Him. It is the voice of love, authority and power. Luke then traces the Lord's family back to Adam, the first man who is called the son of God. Luke uses this genealogy as a backdrop to the coming of the perfect Man coming into this world to do the will of God and bring salvation.

Luke 4 begins with the testing of Jesus by Satan in the wilderness. Just as he did in Genesis chapter 3, Satan questions God. But this time he wasn't challenging the instruction of God to man. He was questioning the relationship between the Father and the Son: "If You are the Son of God". Satan from the beginning of time has destroyed relationships between God and people, husband and wife, parents and children, families, communities and nations. We don't have to look very far to see his work. But there is a relationship he can never damage or destroy: the relationship in the Godhead. We hear the voice of the

Son of God, in all His lowliness and obedience to the Father, asserting the power of the word of God, "But Jesus answered him, saying, 'It is written, "Man shall not live by bread alone, but by every word of God."'" Jesus overcomes the power of the devil by God's word. So, why would we ever doubt it? The first man was disobedient to God in the most beautiful place God created on earth: the garden of Eden. In a wilderness, without any sustenance, Jesus dismisses Satan by the power of His word. At last, a Man who was stronger than Satan was present in this world!

Following this victory, Jesus goes to Nazareth. The Son of God grew up in this despised town. In these few words, "where He had been brought up", Luke describes the greatness of the grace of Christ. He not only entered the world He made, but lived in its poverty. Where does Jesus go first? He goes to the synagogue where the word of God was read. He reads from the book of Isaiah: "The Spirit of the Lord is upon me." The Father's voice has been heard, and the Son's voice was heard. Now the Spirit's voice is heard. The Spirit of God announces Jesus as the preacher of the gospel, the healer of the broken-hearted, the deliverer of captives, the recoverer of sight, the bringer of liberty (Luke 4:18-19). The Holy Spirit has never ceased to glorify the Person of the Son of God.

May the Lord empower us to have a voice in words and actions which witness to who Jesus is, and to be faithful and obedient to the living word of God. May the Holy Spirit of God work in our hearts to demonstrate the love that has redeemed us and seeks to transform us into the likeness of our Saviour. And may we never forget that Satan cannot destroy the relationship into which the love of God has brought us.

Day 32

Wednesday

A cheerful giver

But this I say: He who sows sparingly will also reap sparingly, and he who sows bountifully will also reap bountifully. So let each one give as he purposes in his heart, not grudgingly or of necessity; for God loves a cheerful giver. *(2 Corinthians 9:6-7)*

I had a great affection for John, the brother who married June and me. He and his wife, Gladys, were part of a lovely group of older Christians who cared for us when we were young. We spent many happy hours in their home. John told me that, when he was a young man, he worked on the land. He had the opportunity to get into market gardening. John prayed over what he should do. He was impressed by what he read in Acts 4:36-37: "And Joses, who was also named Barnabas by the apostles (which is translated Son of Encouragement), a Levite of the country of Cyprus, having land, sold it, and brought the money and laid it at the apostles' feet." Based on these verses, John decided not to take the opportunity. He was an intelligent man with ability, but John spent the rest of his life working in ordinary jobs with a simplicity and contentment I always admired.

Even in his nineties, John preached the gospel to passers-by in the open air on Spring Bank in Hull. He died at a great age, and three weeks afterwards his wife, Gladys, went to be with the Lord in her hundredth year. I was privileged to take both funerals. At Gladys's funeral, I told the story their nephew, Bernard, a dear friend of mine, told me. When she was a very old lady, Gladys asked Bernard to a take a gift to a Christian organisation. He handed over a sealed envelope and the brother he gave it to opened the envelope and counted the money to record the amount. It was a considerable sum; such a large sum that Bernard felt he should confirm the amount. He, with the agreement of the brother, rang Gladys's daughter to make sure her aged mother had not made a mistake. There was no mistake. As we walked to the graveside, another friend who had known the family very well drew alongside and thanked me for mentioning the story, then added that it was one of many such occasions.

This lovely couple lived their lives in godliness and contentment. In simplicity and faithfulness, they devoted themselves to following the Lord. They served Him day by day, year by year, for the greater part of a century. Throughout that time, they had been consistent, cheerful givers. John sacrificed the opportunity he had to become a market gardener. But there was no doubt he and Gladys sowed and reaped bountifully. They purposed in their hearts to be lifelong cheerful givers, and God loved them for it. I am so thankful to have known Christians like John and Gladys who gently moved through this world, witnessing to the Saviour and making whatever they had available to Him.

The Lord was a cheerful giver. He ministered in free grace in a world which rejected His goodness. It delights His heart when we bring our freewill offerings from our cheerful hearts. We are to witness cheerfully (Acts 24:10), show mercy cheerfully (Romans 12:8), give cheerfully (2 Corinthians 9:6-7), and worship cheerfully (James 5:13), because we belong to the One who gave Himself for us.

Day 33

Thursday

A cheerful worker

And whatever you do, do it heartily, as to the Lord and not to men, knowing that from the Lord you will receive the reward of the inheritance; for you serve the Lord Christ. (Colossians 3:23-24)

In Colossians 3:23-24 Paul teaches us to regard everyday work as a service for Christ. Work has always had problems. Some people do as little work as possible because they are lazy or do not think they are paid enough. Some work hard only when they are being watched, or try to curry favour with their bosses. People often complain about their occupations and want to be free of them. Others become entirely absorbed in their work and love what they do. Work can be complicated. Paul makes things simple by encouraging Christians to do everything for the Lord.

In the Parable of the Talents in Matthew 25:14-30 I love the way the first two servants approached their master and said, "Lord ... look". There is real joy in their service. They looked forward to bringing to their lord the results of their faithful service. They wanted to please him. And the lord responded joyfully, "Well done, good and faithful servant ... enter into the joy of your lord." Their service was an expression of their relationship. They worked heartily for the lord. And they did not recognise their fellow servant's description of their master as a hard and frightening man. They knew a master who wanted them to succeed in their service and who looked forward to rewarding them.

Some years ago, I was told about a typical young man who never helped around the house. This used to really annoy his sister. He started studying at university, and at end of his first year, he came back home. As soon as the family finished their evening meal, he began clearing the dishes from the table and then started the washing-up. His sister could not believe the change she was seeing. She asked him about his new behaviour. He told her he went along to the Christian Union at university, and had been become a Christian. It was not long before the sister took the same step of faith, and the whole family were led to the Lord. Why? Because a new Christian had the right attitude to work. I doubt anyone told him to wash up. I suspect it was a spontaneous action emerging from the new life he had in Christ. Life doesn't become irksome, but joyful. Wilfulness is changed to willingness and selfishness to selflessness. Christ is formed in us.

The NIV translates verse 23, "Whatever you do, work at it with all your heart, as working for the Lord, not for men." This verse should transform our view of everyday work. It adds dignity to what we do because we serve "the Lord Christ." Paul writes similar words in Ephesians 6:6-7: "doing the will of God from the heart, with goodwill doing service, as to the Lord, and not to men". The Lord Jesus came to do God's perfect will. Before going to the cross, He washed the disciples' feet. In resurrection, the Lord Jesus made breakfast! In the simplest of tasks, He conveyed the most profound spiritual lessons. The apostle saw his work as tentmaker as an essential part of his ministry and witness to fellow Christians. He said to the Ephesian elders, "You yourselves know that these hands have provided for my necessities, and for those who were with me ... Remember the words of the Lord Jesus, that He said, 'It is more blessed to give than to receive.' " (Acts 20:34-35).

Day 34

Friday

Loneliness

Only Luke is with me ... But the Lord stood by me.
(2 Timothy 4:11, 17, ESV)

I have been more and more impressed by the way the apostles had the responsibility to expound the whole counsel of God under the guidance of the Holy Spirit. Their writings lead us into the presence of God and equip us to do His will and to live for Him. Our steps are guided, and our hearts are lifted, by the word of God. It is as relevant and as powerful today as it was when it was first written. What is also so instructive is God's work of grace in the hearts and lives of the writers. Their humanity is not hidden from us. But we can sometimes lose sight of the sacrifices these servants of God made in fulfilling God's will. We have a very poignant insight to this in the final chapter of Paul's letter to his younger co-worker, Timothy.

It is so encouraging to see the relationship with and the spiritual respect Paul had for Timothy. He recognised the need for the next generation of Christians. He ensured that he encouraged and supported them as they took on greater responsibility for the care of the people of God and the burden which that brought. This was so evident in the fatherly love Paul had for Timothy and the value he placed on his friendship and company. His words have added meaning because he had been forsaken by Demas (v. 10). At home, we have been reading about the Kings of Judah. What is so distressing is how many of them began their service so well and ended it so badly. Paul felt the loss of Demas, just as Samuel mourned for Saul. Others of his friends had moved on to fulfil necessary service, like Crescens and Titus.

Paul would miss them, but understood they had responsibility. Yet he felt his loneliness. Service can be a lonely experience. Shepherds need caring for just as much as the flock. He didn't have the comfort of a wife, like Peter, nor did he have children. He had devoted himself entirely to the work of God, and as an ageing saint, he was feeling his weakness and vulnerability.

But then he adds, "Only Luke is with me." Proverbs teaches us about friendship: "But there is a friend who sticks closer than a brother" (Proverbs 18:24). Luke was someone who was always there. We need such friends – friends we can confide in and trust and whose fellowship we enjoy. Paul was a sociable man who valued old friends and who encouraged the next generation. Timothy and Mark had become friends and fellow workers. Paul couldn't wait to see them. June and I always look forward to seeing friends new and old. It is especially joyful when friends turn up unexpectedly. And we have always appreciated friends whose homes you can visit without an invitation; the door is always open.

Paul then speaks of the greatest Friend, Jesus Christ, "But the Lord stood with me and strengthened me." You can feel the apostle's heart being lifted up. He was not alone. The Lord was with him and the Lord strengthened him. You have an immediate sense of what the presence of the Lord meant to the apostle. In these few verses Paul goes from feeling abandoned to abounding in worship at the wonder of His Saviour and Friend (v. 18): "And the Lord will deliver me from every evil work and preserve me for His heavenly kingdom. To Him be glory forever and ever. Amen!"

Day 35

Saturday

Instead of the lad

Now therefore, please let your servant remain instead of the lad as a slave to my lord, and let the lad go up with his brothers.

(Genesis 44:33)

We read about the treatment of Joseph by his brothers in Genesis 37. I once heard someone from the platform rationalising the hatred of Joseph on the grounds of him being a very annoying younger sibling! I understand difficulties arise in large families, and jealousy is a common one. But agreeing to kill your youngest brother, and then changing your mind and selling him into slavery is extreme. No, the real facts are that the brothers of Joseph demonstrate what we are all capable of when consumed by hatred. It was Judah's idea to sell Joseph as a slave (vv. 26-27).

Joseph's life teaches us about what can be in our hearts and what is in God's heart. In Genesis 39 verse 1 we read of Joseph being bought as a slave by Potiphar. Joseph is one of the earliest illustrations of the Lord Jesus in the Old Testament. He is also a powerful example of a man of faith living in the most unjust and adverse circumstances. In verse 2 we are told "The LORD was with Joseph" and blessed all that he did. Joseph is a remarkable example of a theme that runs through the lives of men and women of faith in the Bible. They had the spiritual ability to embrace the circumstances they were confined in as a means to glorify God. It is a theme that has impressed me during lockdown. God blessed Joseph in such circumstances. But when all was going well, Joseph faced an unexpected problem in the form of Potiphar's wife. He addresses it in terms of his responsibility towards God, "How then can I do this great wickedness, and sin against God?" (v. 9). Notice how he takes the challenge to his own heart. The world mocks such thinking. But how much damage, ruin and bitterness have been caused by refusing to take responsibility for our actions before God. Job's wife told her husband in his sickness, "Do you still hold fast to your integrity? Curse God and die!" (Job 2:9). Some would argue that Joseph had every right to ignore the God who had allowed him to be enslaved. But Joseph never lost faith in his God or used his circumstances as an excuse for sin. And it cost him. Instead of being a slave, he became a prisoner. But in prison, "the LORD was with him; and whatever he did, the LORD made it prosper" (v. 23).

From prison, Joseph was raised up by God to rule over Egypt. Later, in this exalted position, Joseph skilfully acted to convict his brothers of their hatred of him. He found it hard to control his emotions when Reuben reminded his brothers of what they did to Joseph (Genesis 42:22-24). In chapter 44 Joseph insists Benjamin remains as a slave in Egypt and the others return home. Then Judah, who was the cause of Joseph's slavery, appeals to Joseph and offers himself as a slave in place of Benjamin. At that moment, Judah understood his sin and sought to redeem his young brother. God worked in his heart, and his action opened the floodgates of Joseph's love for his brothers.

Judah became the tribe of kings, and ultimately the Saviour came out of Judah as the Great Substitute. Joseph resisted sin, and God blessed him. Judah was convicted of his sin and was received in love. May God help us not to give way to sin and also to know, "If we confess our sins, He is faithful and just to forgive us our sins and to cleanse us from all unrighteousness." (1 John 1:9).

Day 36

Sunday

The joy of worship

And they worshipped Him, and returned to Jerusalem with great joy.   *(Luke 24:52)*

When we remember the Lord Jesus, the hymns we sing, the prayers we offer, the scriptures we read, and the thoughts ministered all focus on the Person and the work of Christ. We come as individual believers to bow at the feet of the Lord Jesus Christ and worship, in the words of Paul, "the Son of God who loved me and gave Himself for me." And at the same time, we come in fellowship with other members of the body of Christ to worship the One who "loved the church and gave Himself for her." We ponder in our hearts the journey the Saviour took from glory to the cross of Calvary. We remember His sufferings and the power and glory of His resurrection. With brothers and sisters in Christ, we raise a hymn of praise to the One who died but is now alive forever. Like Mary at the beginning of John 12, these meetings are to be times when the house is "filled with the fragrance of the oil" – in other words, when worship fills the meeting place. And it does not have to be a large meeting. Christ said, "For where two or three are gathered together in My name, I am there in the midst of them" (Matthew 18:20). The Lord Jesus provided the simplest emblems to represent His body and His blood. He also encouraged the smallest groups of His people to meet in His presence to remember Him, valuing each of us.

During these times, the Holy Spirit harmonises our acts of worship. Under His direction, we focus on the many and various aspects of the Lord's Person and work. We can think of the Lord as the Christ of God, the Servant of God, the Son of Man, and the Son of God. And we can think of Him as the Saviour, the Good Shepherd, the Lamb of God, the Lord of Glory. Sometimes a single golden impression of the Lord runs through our worship. At other times the Spirit of God blends several thoughts together. But, fundamentally, there is a response of love to the Saviour who gave Himself for us. What is central to these acts of worship is what the Lord asks us to do: to remember Him. This remembrance focuses on the sacrifice of Himself in the bread and wine. He gave these emblems meaning because He never wanted us to lose the sense of the depth of His love for us. As we remember Him, we look up to where He is now: "But this Man, after He had offered one sacrifice for sins forever, sat down at the right hand of God" (Hebrews 10:12).

Revelation 5 presents the Lord Jesus as a Lamb, bearing the marks of sacrifice. The Lamb receives the praise and worship of the whole of creation. In the physical and spiritual realms, every knee bows and every tongue confesses the worthiness of the Lamb. The love expressed by the Lord's giving of Himself is the ground of all the purposes of God. It is love which cannot be fathomed. The thrill of worship never ceases. In Acts 1:11 the angels tell the disciples that this same Jesus will come again. Paul writes that "as often as you eat this bread and drink this cup, you proclaim the Lord's death till He comes" (1 Corinthians 11:26). Luke also writes at the end of his gospel that the disciples returned from witnessing the Lord's ascension into heaven in glory, with "great joy" in their hearts. Whenever we come and pour out our worship remembering the Lord Jesus, He fills our hearts with Himself. He always sends us out to serve Him, full of the joy of His salvation.

Day 37

Monday

Lifting up holy hands

I desire therefore that the men pray everywhere, lifting up holy hands, without wrath and doubting. (1 Timothy 2:8)

But Moses' hands became heavy; so they took a stone and put it under him, and he sat on it. And Aaron and Hur supported his hands, one on one side, and the other on the other side; and his hands were steady until the going down of the sun. So Joshua defeated Amalek and his people with the edge of the sword.
(Exodus 17:12-13)

We recently restarted our local prayer meeting by Zoom. It is so encouraging to be able to pray together. I remember, as a young Christian, going to the prayer meeting for the first time. We started with a hymn, and afterwards, when the first brother started to pray, everyone got down on their knees. It was a hard floor to kneel on. But as we knelt down, so our hearts rose up to the Throne of Grace in heaven. As in marriage, those who pray together stay together, so praying together binds the people of God together. Paul speaks about "lifting up holy hands". The expression conveys stretching out in an appeal to God from lives which seek to walk in His paths of righteousness. We don't come with anger and discontentment in our hearts. And we don't come doubting. We approach God as the recipients of His mercy and His glorious grace, and we come in faith. The Lord Jesus invites us to ask in His name and assures us we will be heard.

The battle between Israel and Amalek was decided on a hill above the battlefield. Three men went to the top of the hill: Moses, Aaron the brother of Moses, and their friend Hur. Moses held up the rod of God and Joshua prevailed in the battle. But as he tired, he could not keep his hand raised, and Amalek became stronger. So Aaron and Hur found a rock for Moses to sit on and they supported his hands, one on the left, and the other on the right. This fellowship of intercession defeated Amalek.

This miraculous event is a vivid illustration of intercessory prayer. Moses took the responsibility to act on behalf of others. Prayer demands time, energy and commitment. We need to bring our families, fellow believers and many others to the Throne of Grace. This holy activity can become too heavy for us. We can become disheartened and discouraged. Sometimes we can feel that God isn't answering our prayers. But we have two advocates who are far greater than Moses, Aaron and Hur who come to our aid: our risen Saviour and the indwelling Holy Spirit of God. Their strength is never diminished, their ears and eyes are never closed, and their work of intercession never ceases. They know our weakness, and they come to our aid. So never let us despair, but pray without ceasing.

"Likewise the Spirit also helps in our weaknesses. For we do not know what we should pray for as we ought, but the Spirit Himself makes intercession for us with groanings which cannot be uttered. Now He who searches the hearts knows what the mind of the Spirit is, because He makes intercession for the saints according to the will of God ... Who is he who condemns? It is Christ who died, and furthermore is also risen, who is even at the right hand of God, who also makes intercession for us" (Romans 8:26-27, 34).

Day 38

Tuesday

The shortest verses and sayings

Jesus wept … Father, I thank You. *(John 11:35, 41)*

John 11 teaches us profound lessons about human suffering and the heart of God. The chapter begins with a message, "Lord, behold, he whom You love is sick" (v. 3). The family knew that the Lord loved them, and this is confirmed in verse 5, "Jesus loved Martha and her sister and Lazarus." There is no doubt about the love of Christ and, at the same time, there is no doubt about the bitterness of the circumstances when Jesus declares, "Lazarus is dead."

What follows is a unique record of the feelings and actions of the Son of God amid sorrow, grief and death. Jesus promises Martha that Lazarus will rise again, and Martha expressed her belief in the future resurrection. Jesus uses this conversation to declare that He is the "resurrection and the life" (v. 25). Martha responds in faith from her heart, "Yes, Lord, I believe that You are the Christ, the Son of God, who is to come into the world." Martha's heart was broken: her faith in the Lord was not.

When Mary appears, she falls in distress at the Lord's feet. The overwhelming and genuine sorrow that filled her heart and those who surrounded the Lord Jesus caused the Lord of Glory to weep. It is a moment which brings home to our hearts the love of the Lord as we pass through the pain of loss in our lives. But it was not only the tears of the Lord but also the inner groaning which expressed His depth of feeling. This groaning at the same time described His preparation to act in power as He orders the rolling away of the stone at the tomb of Lazarus.

The Lord's tears and groaning were not the final emotions of the Lord as He was about to demonstrate His power over death. The Lord lifted His heart in thankfulness to the Father. In the same way, when He later instituted the Lord's Supper, before breaking the bread which speaks of His perfect sacrifice, He gave thanks. It was with a heart of thankfulness that the Lord says, "Lazarus, come forth!"

There is a day coming, for which we groan, when "God will wipe away every tear from their eyes; there shall be no more death, nor sorrow, nor crying. There shall be no more pain, for the former things have passed away" (Revelation 21:4). That day has not come. And we are subject to the distress and sorrow which so profoundly affects our lives now. But we do have the assurance of the Lord's presence, love and power to carry us through such circumstances. When Jesus raised Lazarus, He called him by name. Our hope looks forward to a day when the Lord will call us by name into His presence. His love will reign eternally. Now day by day, we are sustained by the One who is the resurrection and the life.

The shortest verses in the Bible teach us so much. Because "Jesus wept" we know His love. Because Jesus cried, "Finished", we know His eternal salvation. Now He wants us to know joy: "Rejoice evermore" (1 Thessalonians 5:16, AV).

Day 39

Wednesday

The simplicity of Sychar: humility in witnessing

So He came to a city of Samaria which is called Sychar, near the plot of ground that Jacob gave to his son Joseph. Now Jacob's well was there. Jesus therefore, being wearied from His journey, sat thus by the well. It was about the sixth hour. (John 4:5-6)

Many times in the Gospels, we read of the Lord intervening in grace in the lives of men and women. But at Sychar's well, the Lord teaches us, in the simplicity and ordinariness of an everyday event, His power to lead one person who was in deep need to Himself. At the same time, we learn from Him how to communicate our faith in Christ. I remember reading about an evangelist who prayed each day that he would have at least one opportunity to witness to the Lord Jesus. But when such opportunities present themselves, how do we take advantage of them? John explains that Jesus was weary as He sat resting from His journey. We are not usually at our best when we are tired and hungry, and the day is hot. But the Lord uses such circumstances to start a conversation with a woman who came to draw water. In doing so, He teaches us to always be ready to take advantage of everyday situations to speak about spiritual matters. Generally, we have no difficulty talking to people we meet about the weather, the Government, lockdown, family, and lots more. But it is difficult to speak about the Saviour. Of course, we can be very direct and jump straight in, almost blurting out the gospel, or we may give some helpful literature. Thank God, the Lord uses these endeavours.

But the Lord at Sychar shows us how to make a commonplace experience special. He teaches us that communicating the things of God should be a natural process. So He starts the conversation by asking for a drink. First of all, the Lord puts Himself in the position of needing something rather than giving something. But He also knew that His simple request would create interest and surprise – and it did: "'How is it that You, being a Jew, ask a drink from me, a Samaritan woman?' For Jews have no dealings with Samaritans."

As Christians, our humility in words and actions should be surprising, and attract the interest and attention of the people we meet. The humility of the Lord immediately drew the woman into a conversation which would transform her life.

But that conversation did not seem to start well. Straightaway, the woman raised barriers. We should not be surprised when people erect barriers or challenge our faith. These obstacles are often defences behind which people hide their spiritual need. The Lord had asked for a drink of water so He could give her salvation, "If you knew the gift of God, and who it is who says to you, 'Give Me a drink,' you would have asked Him, and He would have given you living water" (v. 10). He takes her on a journey into life. In doing so, Jesus shows us how to witness to Him in a world He describes as "already white for harvest!" (v. 35). He encourages us to watch Him, the greatest soul-winner, and learn how to minister His grace and love in a world which so much needs Him.

Day 40

Thursday

The simplicity of Sychar: patience and kindness in witnessing

The woman said to Him, "Sir, You have nothing to draw with, and the well is deep. Where then do You get that living water?"

(John 4:11)

We live in a fast-talking world that loves to communicate quickly and by a variety of means, but so often at a superficial level. We rarely have time to sit and reflect on our existence. At Sychar's well, everything was slowed down as the Lord step by step leads the woman at the well to Himself. Let us pray for these kinds of moments, when ordinary conversations can be developed, to allow time to patiently communicate the Gospel.

The woman at the well did not immediately understand what the Lord was speaking about: "Sir, You have nothing to draw with, and the well is deep. Where then do You get that living water? Are You greater than our father Jacob, who gave us the well, and drank from it himself, as well as his sons and his livestock?" (vv. 11-12). Questions and misunderstandings are opportunities. Today there is a lot of ignorance of the Bible and its message, and especially of the Saviour. The Lord was both patient and persistent in His conversation with the woman. He presented to her a joyous life she did not possess: "Jesus answered and said to her, 'Whoever drinks of this water will thirst again, but whoever drinks of the water that I shall give him will never thirst. But the water that I shall give him will become in him a fountain of water springing up into everlasting life'" (vv. 13-14). He moves her thoughts from her physical life to spiritual life. And He illustrates this with object lessons from her experience as she drew water each day. He relates to her circumstances, and He explains in pictures. The Lord frequently communicated profound messages through simple illustrations. We should do the same.

There is a turning point in the Lord's conversation when the woman asks, "Sir, give me this water, that I may not thirst, nor come here to draw." It is also the point when, in grace, the Lord challenges the woman's life by saying, "Go, call your husband, and come here" (v. 16). The woman simply answers, "I have no husband." This is a very striking moment. It was not just the Lord's words which impressed the woman: it was His person. John Wesley said, "Let your words be the genuine picture of your heart." This was so true of the Lord. We need to understand that people respond, not merely to our words, but to who we are. The woman felt she could confide in the Lord. And she is amazed when the Lord says, "You have well said, 'I have no husband,' for you have had five husbands, and the one whom you now have is not your husband; in that you spoke truly" (vv. 17-18).

We must never forget that we do not witness alone. The Lord has the power, not only to guide what we say and how we say it, but at the same time He can also work in the hearts and minds of those we want to lead to Him. This critical point of confidence is so important. I have discovered over the years that people who are often resentful of God, for whatever reason, eventually can take the opportunity to speak seriously about spiritual matters.

The woman discovered someone who was a Jew and a prophet. She expected to be condemned and judged by such a person. Instead, she found someone who cared for her soul. She was about to discover Christ. May the Lord teach us to care for the souls of others and look to lead them, by His grace, to Himself.

Day 41

Friday

The simplicity of Sychar: the focus of witnessing

"But the hour is coming, and now is, when the true worshippers will worship the Father in spirit and truth; for the Father is seeking such to worship Him. God is Spirit, and those who worship Him must worship in spirit and truth." (John 4:23-24)

We have discovered how the woman at the well responded to the graciousness of the Lord's appeal to her. For several years, at lunchtime, I used to walk into a town centre close to the offices where I worked. What surprised me was the way many people spoke to each and their children in everyday conversation. There was frequently a crudeness of expression which had obviously become a habitual way of talking. I don't think the people who used that language ever considered how they spoke, or even cared. We read of the Lord that "grace is poured upon Your lips" (Psalm 45:2). And part of our testimony is to use the power of gracious words.

It is also interesting that the woman tried to turn her conversation with the Lord towards religious differences. When people talk about spiritual things, they naturally turn to their own experience of religion. The distinction the woman made between the Jews and the Samaritans was genuine. The history of Christendom is also scarred by divisions and sub-divisions. These events have driven people away from God and each other. But the Lord puts religion to one side and focuses on the worship of the Father. In the previous chapter, Jesus says to Nicodemus, a sincere and spiritual man, "You must be born again" (John 3:7). Jesus speaks to the nameless woman by the well about worshipping the Father. People at their very best still need the salvation of Christ to become the children of God. People who are so far from God, through the same salvation in Christ, can be brought near to the God who loves us and gave His Son for our redemption. We receive life, and in that life we can come in "the beauty of holiness" (Psalm 29:2) to worship the Father from our hearts in spirit and truth.

When the woman arrived at Sychar's well, she did not know the stranger sitting close by was the Christ, the Son of God. The Lord spoke to her in grace and led her out of spiritual and moral darkness into salvation. He took her into a place of acceptance and nearness. He stripped away the emptiness of religion, even that which had been established by God in Jerusalem. The Lord leads her beyond religion and earth to the Person of the Father in heaven.

You have the impression when the Lord meets the woman at Sychar's well that no-one else was there. Perhaps she deliberately went to the well when it was quiet. But the Lord knew she would come, and He waited for her so He could say to her, "But the hour is coming, and now is, when the true worshippers will worship the Father in spirit and truth; for the Father is seeking such to worship Him. God is Spirit, and those who worship Him must worship in spirit and truth." It was then the woman said, "I know that Messiah is coming … When He comes, He will tell us all things." Jesus replied, "I who speak to you am He" and the light of His Person shines into her heart. It was a light she could not keep to herself: "Come see a Man who told me all things that I ever did." She declares the wonder of God's salvation through Christ, which takes us out of darkness into His marvellous light and encourages us to share our experience of His love with others.

Day 42

Saturday

The simplicity of Sychar: the joy of witnessing

"Behold, I say to you, lift up your eyes and look at the fields, for they are already white for harvest!" *(John 4:35)*

The disciples were surprised that the Lord was in conversation with the woman at the well, but kept their thoughts to themselves. The Lord's actions of grace were often judged, and even the disciples failed to understand when the Lord was engaged in seeking the lost. We must never lose sight of the grace of God. It reached us in all our need, and it should always influence our thoughts and actions towards others.

The woman left her water pot. The Spirit of God seems to use this simple act to emphasise what the woman had found in Christ. It signalled the end of an old life and the beginning of a new one. She went straight into the town and witnessed, not to the women, but to the men. The Lord did not tell her to do this directly. The new life she possessed compelled her to share what she had discovered. It was a powerful, personal and straightforward witness: "Come, see a Man who told me all things that I ever did. Could this be the Christ?" Her witness was similar to that of Andrew and Philip in John 1. When she said, "Could this be the Christ?", she was not expressing doubt but inviting others to discover the Saviour for themselves. What an effect she had: "And many of the Samaritans of that city believed in Him because of the word of the woman who testified, 'He told me all that I ever did.'" The Samaritans urged the Lord to stay with them, and over the following two days many more people believed in Christ as the Saviour of the world. It is no surprise that, when Philip the evangelist arrives in Samaria in Acts 8, there is such an overwhelming response to the gospel. We rarely consider the foundational work the Lord did in seeking the lost through His wonderful ministry and its connection with the harvest that the apostles reaped in Jerusalem, Judea and Samaria.

It was this future ministry the Lord spoke to the disciples of when they encouraged Him to have something to eat and He responds with the words, "I have food to eat of which you do not know." The disciples often struggled to connect with the Lord's thoughts. And He has to explain, "My food is to do the will of Him who sent Me, and to finish His work." He wanted the disciples to understand the importance of doing God's will in evangelism, and He describes this in terms of a harvest. Despite all the rejection the Lord endured in this world, He saw a glorious harvest. He later speaks of Himself as a grain of wheat falling into the ground and dying, but as a result, bringing forth "much fruit" (John 12:24). The joy the Lord had in drawing the woman at the well to Himself was a token of the immense joy He would have in the vast company of the redeemed.

This should encourage us in our prayer for and our engagement in evangelism. The joy of God is the great theme of salvation (Luke 15). By the well, in despised Samaria, the Lord had the joy of finding another lost sheep. His shepherd's heart has never changed. And today He still says to us, "Lift up your eyes and look at the fields, for they are already white for harvest!" The work of salvation is entirely His, but He encourages us to be actively and joyfully involved in sharing the "good tidings of great joy" (Luke 2:10).

Day 43

Sunday

Bethany, where heaven is open

And He led them out as far as Bethany, and He lifted up His hands and blessed them. Now it came to pass, while He blessed them, that He was parted from them and carried up into heaven. And they worshipped Him, and returned to Jerusalem with great joy, and were continually in the temple praising and blessing God. Amen. (Luke 24:50-53)

The Lord never stops being the Shepherd. Luke closes his gospel with the short journey to Bethany: "He led them out as far as Bethany." The Lord was welcomed and worshipped in this small town. In it, we learn so much about the grace and love of our Saviour. We discover the importance of sitting quietly in His presence and listening to His voice. He values our company. In Martha's home, we learn that He understands all the cares and anxieties that trouble us, and wants us to cast our care upon Him (1 Peter 5:7). In Bethany, we know His love for each one of us: "Now Jesus loved Martha and her sister and Lazarus" (John 11:5). In the deep pain caused by the death of Lazarus, we discover the sympathy and the power of the One who is "the resurrection and the life" (John 11:25).

In John 12, through a simple meal at Bethany, we are taught

 – to place the Lord at the centre of our lives: "There they made Him a supper."

 – Jesus is central to our service: "Martha served."

 – He is the focus of our fellowship: "Lazarus was one of those who sat at the table with Him."

– the Lord is the object of our worship: "Then Mary took a pound of very costly oil of spikenard, anointed the feet of Jesus, and wiped His feet with her hair. And the house was filled with the fragrance of the oil."

Jerusalem, the great city, should have lifted up its gates to welcome the King of Glory:

> Lift up your heads, O you gates!
> And be lifted up, you everlasting doors!
> And the King of glory shall come in (Psalm 24:7).

In John 19 Pilate presented Jesus to the hate-filled crowd in Jerusalem with the words, "Behold your King!" Their reply was, "Away with Him, away with Him! Crucify Him!" Pilate asked them, "Shall I crucify your King?" And the spiritual leaders of God's people answered, "We have no king but Caesar!" Then Jesus, as the Lamb of God, was led away to Calvary (vv. 14-16).

The Lord is no longer in this world as the lowly Nazarene. He is risen and glorified. But this morning, from heaven, as our Shepherd, He leads us to a quiet place – a place away from the world which crucified the Son of God. His hands, which were nailed to the cross, are lifted up in blessing. We see the One who was lifted up between heaven and earth, now crowned with glory and honour in heaven. The Flock of God gives its responses to an opened heaven in joyful worship to the Son of God who loved the church and gave Himself for her. We have fellowship with the Father and the Son in the power and liberty of the Holy Spirit (1 John 1:3-4).

From this place of worship, we return to our everyday circumstances and responsibilities. We do so with joy in our hearts, a hope that transforms our lives, and a love that tells the world that we belong to the Lord Jesus Christ.

Day 44

Monday

Turning the world the right way up

Remembering without ceasing your work of faith, labour of love, and patience of hope in our Lord Jesus Christ in the sight of our God and Father. (1 Thessalonians 1:3)

After God's remarkable work in Philippi (Acts 16), Paul and Silas travelled to Thessalonica. In the synagogue, over three Sabbaths, they explained and proved from the word of God the necessity of Christ's suffering and death, and declared His resurrection. As a result, a work of God began in the hearts of the godly Jews and devout Greeks, including some eminent women. Persecution followed, and Paul and Silas were accused of "turning the world upside down". The brethren took the apostles to safety in Berea. There they found noble Jews who received the word of God eagerly and searched the Scriptures daily to discover the truth of what Paul and Silas were teaching. Again, there was blessing, before troublemakers arrived from Thessalonica, and the brethren once more protected Paul by taking him to Athens.

Afterwards, Paul writes to the young church in Thessalonica to encourage them, knowing they would be under attack from those who opposed the Gospel. It is remarkable the way God blessed these early churches. The apostles were often only with these new believers for a short time. But the speed of the spiritual growth of these early Christians was astonishing. Sometimes we can forget the way that God protects, builds and blesses His people. God saves, establishes and keeps those He loves, despite opposition. Paul and Silas were accused of "turning the world upside down". They didn't. They turned it "the right way up"! And the characteristics of this right-way-up living were manifested by the faith, love and hope of the young Thessalonian Christians.

Their faith was immediately demonstrated by their works. We see this clearly in the way they care for Paul and Silas, ensuring they are protected by standing in love between them and those who would do them harm. Faith in the Saviour leads to faith expressed in our lives by good works. Faith in Christ is linked to the love of Christ. Paul writes of their labour of love. "Labour" describes the exercise of spiritual energy and the ceaseless effort that holds nothing back. Their faith and love were also underpinned by a living hope in the Lord Jesus Christ. It was a patient hope that was not undermined by difficult circumstances but which sustained them victoriously in such difficulties. These young Thessalonian Christians had life in Christ and expressed it fully because, in the words of Paul, they were "loved by God" (v. 4, ESV).

Paul describes, in what is widely agreed to be his first letter to a church, the three attributes: faith, love and hope. In doing so he used the example of the young Thessalonian church to encourage generations of Christians. The length of time we have been Christians should never diminish our faith, love and hope. Instead, it should increase these central features of Christianity in our lives. We are loved by God, and He has given all that we need to work in faith as people who are zealous of good works. God's love has been poured into our hearts, enabling us to pour out the same love in service to Him. And our living hope in Christ can carry us through every challenge we face, knowing that "all things work together for good to those who love God, to those who are called according to His purpose" (Romans 8:28).

Day 45

Tuesday

Turning, serving and waiting

For from you the word of the Lord has sounded forth, not only in Macedonia and Achaia, but also in every place. Your faith toward God has gone out, so that we do not need to say anything. For they themselves declare concerning us what manner of entry we had to you, and how you turned to God from idols to serve the living and true God, and to wait for His Son from heaven.

(1 Thessalonians 1:8-9)

Persecution swiftly followed the blessing of the Gospel in Thessalonica, and it followed Paul and Silas to Berea. But instead of this persecution restricting the further blessing of the Gospel, the opposite happened. The Thessalonian church became central to spreading the word of God throughout Macedonia and Achaia, and beyond. This is so encouraging.

Paul highlights another three features which marked the testimony of these young Christians. First, they turned to God from idols. If you read Paul's visit to Thessalonica in Acts 17, you will see that the first people who trusted in Christ were godly Jews and devout Greeks. This angered the orthodox and influential Jews in the city and led to a public outcry and the persecution which followed. Paul now writes about something not recorded in Acts 17 – what happened next. Instead of the Gospel being confined, it advanced. The Lord tells us in Matthew 16:18, "I will build My church, and the gates of Hades shall not prevail against it." He proved this in Macedonia. Through the Gospel, people turned to God from idols. There was no doubt about their salvation. They were changed. Idolatry was endemic in the world Paul knew and affected daily life. The power of the Gospel delivered people from its hold and transformed their lives. No wonder that, when Christianity became more widespread, John writes his timeless warning, "Little children keep yourselves from idols." Idols may have changed in appearance, but we always need to be aware of the real spiritual damage they pose.

The Thessalonians served the "living and true God". Their faith had turned them to God, and His love motivated their service – their work of faith and labour of love. Their lives were no longer governed by the worship of created, material idols. Instead, they were a new creation in Christ Jesus, and their testimony was the reversal of a world corrupted by people who "exchanged the truth of God for the lie, and worshipped and served the creature rather than the Creator, who is blessed forever. Amen" (Romans 1:25). The Thessalonians worshipped and served the one true God and powerfully witnessed to Him in their lives.

Finally, they waited for the return of Christ. This hope in the Lord developed their faith, motivated their love, and paced and focussed their lives. They lived in anticipation of Christ's return. This was not a vague, future promise: it was a vivid, daily incentive to live fruitful lives for God. Just as the windows of Daniel's house in Babylon were always opened towards Jerusalem, so their hearts were always "looking unto Jesus, the author and finisher of our faith" and "looking for the blessed hope and glorious appearing of our great God and Saviour Jesus Christ". Centuries have not faded that hope, but brought its fulfilment closer.

Day 46

Wednesday

Spiritual parenting

But we were gentle among you, just as a nursing mother cherishes her own children ... you know how we exhorted, and comforted, and charged every one of you, as a father does his own children, that you would walk worthy of God who calls you into His own kingdom and glory. (1 Thessalonians 2:7,11-12)

It is good to read Paul's letters with reference to the records of his missionary journeys in the Acts of the Apostles. We are given a comprehensive view of the ministry he and his fellow workers undertook. It helps us understand the deep spiritual, emotional and physical commitment they had to the work of God, and their genuine love for Christ's Church. This is all the more powerful when you consider the work in Thessalonica began as Paul and Silas were recovering from the brutal treatment they received at Philippi. Their boldness in the Gospel was not blunted and they did not flinch in the face of fresh conflict. Paul and Silas had been entrusted with the gospel and they faithfully, sincerely and selflessly preached it. Even though they had the right to be supported as the servants of God, they insisted on supporting themselves.

This character of self-sacrifice is highlighted in the characteristics of the spiritual parenting he writes about. The parent's love and influence are placed in the order you expect them to be in. We see this first in verse 7: "But we were gentle among you, just as a nursing mother cherishes her own children." In their immaturity of faith these young believers at Thessalonica needed to know Christ's gentleness and care as a bedrock for their spiritual development. It is interesting that it was from the homes of the Philippian jailer and Lydia that Paul and Silas left Philippi to travel to Thessalonica. I suspect Lydia was always marked by gentleness and care. But the jailer was instantaneously transformed into a gentle and caring man (see the end of Acts 16). Knowing the gentleness of Christ makes us gentle people. This does not mean we are weak and ineffectual, but we are empowered to support and help others.

This power was seen as Paul related how he and his friends shared and lived out the Gospel in sacrificial service and hard work to ensure they were not a burden to those they served. They were totally committed to building up the new church in Thessalonica. And as spiritual fathers they provided exhortation and comfort, and also charged their spiritual children to live for the glory of God. Spiritual fathers exhort in terms of calling their children to learn, progress, and fulfil their spiritual potential. At the same time they comfort and encourage them when they are challenged and things get tough. Exhortation and comfort work in harmony to help children grow and mature. And, as fathers, they also charge or implore their children to take responsibility to live lives worthy of the God who had called them into His kingdom and given them the hope of glory.

The example of the apostles brings home to us the cost and the joy of committing ourselves to the ministry of Christ in the Gospel, and the building up of His Church. It is a cost worth paying and a joy worth knowing.

Day 47

Thursday

Spiritual shepherding

And may the Lord make you increase and abound in love to one another and to all, just as we do to you, so that He may establish your hearts blameless in holiness before our God and Father at the coming of our Lord Jesus Christ with all His saints.

(1 Thessalonians 3:12-13)

The early chapters of 1 Thessalonians teach us about caring for the people of God and the characteristics of spiritually shepherding them. We see this in the depth of concern Paul had toward the young church at Thessalonica. Today's chapter also teaches us about the confidence Paul had in his co-workers, in this particular instance, Timothy. This is a lesson we can easily pass over. In Mark 6:7 the Lord sent His disciples out two by two. We see Peter and John placed together, also Andrew and Philip. In the missionary work in the book of Acts, Paul worked with Barnabas, then with Silas and, as we see today, Timothy. Fellowship in the service of God generally, and shepherding His people particularly, is essential. This includes preparing the next generation for this ministry. This doesn't mean the servants were always side by side, but it does mean their service was done in harmony.

Paul never saw himself as indispensable. He valued and encouraged gift and potential in others. He describes Timothy as a brother, a minister of God, and a fellow worker in the Gospel of Christ. As a brother, we see his responsibility in the church; as a minister of God, we see his responsibility before God; and as a co-worker in the Gospel, we see his responsibility in the world. Timothy demonstrated his faithfulness in these areas. He established and encouraged the Thessalonians in their faith because he had been established and encouraged in his own faith. He was not sent out unprepared. By being shepherded, he became a shepherd.

In sending Timothy to Thessalonica, Paul was not relinquishing his concern for those he brought to Christ: he was fulfilling it. As a spiritual shepherd, he cared for the flock and felt their need in his own heart. He reacted to this need by sending Timothy. When Timothy returned to tell Paul about the good news of the Thessalonians' work of faith, labour of love, and steadfast hope, the apostle was overjoyed. And what especially touched him was the affection they had towards him personally. This helps us to understand how the Flock of God develops. The work of spiritual shepherding begins with an understanding of the preciousness of the people of God to Christ. It is a service of love which always acts selflessly for the good of God's people. It generates mutual love. It is done in fellowship with others and under the guidance the Lord Jesus Christ, our Good, Great and Chief Shepherd. The work is marked by genuine concern, loving action, intercession, thankfulness, and stimulates the ability and gift of others. The aim is to see the people of God, both standing fast and growing in the grace of our Lord Jesus Christ.

Paul worked tirelessly to shepherd the people of God. He also developed servants of God like Timothy to continue this work. But above all, he understood it was only through dependence upon our God and Father, the Lord Jesus Christ and the power of the Holy Spirit that this work could be accomplished to God's glory and our blessing.

Day 48

Friday

Spiritual home

And so we will always be with the Lord. (1 Thessalonians 4:17, ESV)

Paul begins 1 Thessalonians 4 by exhorting his fellow believers to live sanctified lives for God. Holiness was to mark them as Christians, and, as Paul writes in Philippians, they were to be "children of God without fault in the midst of a crooked and perverse generation, among whom you shine as lights in the world" (Philippians 2:15). The apostle is very direct in warning them about immorality and its damaging effects.

Paul bears testimony to the evidence that they had been taught by God to love one another. This was seen locally and throughout Macedonia. It was something the apostle urged them to continue in and to develop more and more. Interestingly, Paul encourages them to "aspire" to lead a quiet life, to mind their own business, and to work with their own hands. He highlights the powerful testimony before God of peaceful, discreet, hard-working Christians as something to be pursued and a vital part of our witness as the people of God: "And what does the LORD require of you / But to do justly, / To love mercy, / And to walk humbly with your God?" (Micah 6:8). In the first section of today's chapter, the apostle encouraged them to continue in their "work of faith and labour of love", referred to in the opening chapter. Then he turns to the subject of the "patience of hope in our Lord Jesus Christ" (1:3).

Paul wanted them to be clear about the coming of the Lord Jesus Christ. The Lord speaks of this in John 14:3: "I will come again…" and the angels announce it in Acts 1:11: "This same

Jesus, who was taken up from you into heaven, will so come in like manner as you saw Him go into heaven." In the final section of our chapter today, the apostle describes this event in greater detail. He does this to comfort the hearts of those concerned about Christians who had died. We believe that Jesus died for us and rose again for our salvation. He is the resurrection and the life. Paul teaches, "by the word of the Lord" (v. 15), that, when Jesus returns for His people, His first act is to raise the bodies of the vast company of those who have died in Christ. The dead in Christ rise first (v. 16). These are then joined by Christians alive on earth. Together they meet the Lord in the air. Paul then adds those beautiful words, "And so we will always be with the Lord" (v. 17, ESV). The Lord prayed in John 17:24, "Father, I desire that they also whom You gave Me may be with Me where I am, that they may behold My glory which You have given Me; for You loved Me before the foundation of the world."

This week I spoke at the graveside of a dear old friend, Hazel, whom I had known for over 50 years. There was a freezing wind and it was raining as we stood around the open grave. But we were not sad. Instead, a deep joy filled our hearts because our sister was already with the Lord: "to depart and be with Christ, which is far better" (Philippians 1:23). One of the Scriptures I read was Revelation 4:1, where the apostle is invited into heaven with the words, "Come up here." The Lord came down here so that one day He could say to us, "Come up here." This is our hope in Him, and we believe it with all our hearts. God's love will not be satisfied until we are brought by our Saviour into His Father's home: "And so we will always be with the Lord."

Day 49

Saturday

Spiritual life

Now may the God of peace Himself sanctify you completely; and may your whole spirit, soul, and body be preserved blameless at the coming of our Lord Jesus Christ. (1 Thessalonians 5:23)

In the final part of chapter 4 Paul taught the Thessalonians about the "Rapture", when the Lord comes for His people. In chapter 5 he speaks about the Day of the Lord. This refers to Jesus Christ coming as the "King of kings, and Lord of lords" to begin His millennial reign. Paul had already explained that this day would come "as a thief in the night". The "Rapture" is an act of love. The Day of the Lord is an act of righteousness. This world has been administered by humankind for thousands of years. Today we see the spiritual, moral, physical, political, and economic damage unrighteousness has caused. You don't have to be a Christian to understand how deeply human behaviour has hurt us, or recognise the overwhelming power of materialism and corruption. Paul writes in Romans 8:22 about the "groan" of creation. Here he writes about the day God intervenes in His creation, not in the lowly grace of Jesus, but in the power of the One whose name is above every name – the same Jesus. It is the day, at last, when righteousness will reign over the earth:

> "The Sun of Righteousness shall arise
> With healing in His wings" (Malachi 4:2).

It is God's business to deal with the world in its entirety. Our responsibility is to live as "sons of light and sons of the day" (v. 5). We are not to sleepwalk unaffected through the world but to live for God in the circumstances He has placed us. We are to watch out for ourselves and others. To be sober means to be sound in mind. We are to have the mind of Christ; this is displayed in the protection and power of faith, love and the hope of salvation (vv. 6-8). Paul connects again to their "work of faith and labour of love" in chapter 1. Then he reminds them of the glorious facts that Jesus Christ "died for us" and we will "live together with Him", which links to their "patience of hope in our Lord Jesus Christ" (1:3).

In the meantime, we are to live in the power of our great salvation. The people of God should recognise, support and love those who care for the flock of God. Peace should govern our relationships. The people of God are to be cared for in a variety of circumstances. Some need to be warned of unspiritual behaviour, those who are despondent need encouragement, and we are to support the weak, however weakness manifests itself. One of the great features of the body of Christ is its inclusiveness. Our patience and longsuffering should be extended to all the Lord's people. We should never seek revenge but always the good of all. Paul wanted joy, prayerfulness and thankfulness to be features which characterised the Thessalonians. For this to happen, we must not put out the fire of God's Spirit in our hearts or in the hearts of others, but stimulate those things which cause "our heart burn within us". The Spirit through the word of God brings Christ to our hearts (Luke 24:32). By the same Holy Spirit and word of God we are to test all things, uphold what is good and distance ourselves from evil. It is the God of peace who keeps us separate from evil whilst empowering us to do good in anticipation of the day of the Lord, when the Lord Jesus Christ will reign, not only in our hearts, but in this world.

Day 50

Sunday

Sanctified life

Now may the God of peace Himself sanctify you completely; and may your whole spirit, soul, and body be preserved blameless at the coming of our Lord Jesus Christ. (1 Thessalonians 5:23)

I would like to return to what is essentially a prayer of Paul at the end of his letter to the Thessalonians. In Hebrews 13 we read, "Now may the God of peace who brought up our Lord Jesus from the dead, that great Shepherd of the sheep, through the blood of the everlasting covenant, make you complete in every good work to do His will, working in you what is well pleasing in His sight, through Jesus Christ, to whom be glory forever and ever. Amen" (vv. 20-21). The Lord Jesus Christ died for us, and the God of peace in righteousness raised Him up.

> Mercy and truth have met together;
> Righteousness and peace have kissed (Psalm 85:10)

The God of peace wants us to know His presence (Philippians 4:9) and the sanctification it produces.

Sanctification involves separation to God and separation from evil in all its forms. It is about holiness, and equips us for the worship and service of God. It produces Christlikeness. And it affects the whole of our beings, spirit, soul and body. Our spirit is that invisible part of us that makes us conscious of God and able to communicate with Him. Our soul embraces our emotions and personalities. Our bodies physically express who we are. Together they describe our whole being. We were made by God to have fellowship with God. When sin separated people from God, how did God bring about salvation? By entering His creation in the Person of Jesus Christ. In the words of Philippians 2, He came "in the likeness of men". The Lord Jesus took a body:

> Therefore, when He came into the world, He said:
> "Sacrifice and offering You did not desire,
> But a body You have prepared for Me" (Hebrews 10:5).

In His body, He expressed the fullness of God's love and grace, and it was His body that was given for us. The Lord Jesus expressed His holy deep emotions in His soul: "Now My soul is troubled, and what shall I say? 'Father, save Me from this hour'? But for this purpose I came to this hour" (John 12:27). And the last words Jesus spoke on the cross were addressed to His Father at the moment He laid down His life for our redemption: "Father, 'into Your hands I commit My spirit'" (Luke 23:46).

The Lord devoted Himself, body, soul and spirit, to the Father's will and to accomplish the work of salvation. Now, as the redeemed people of God, we are enabled to respond to God in the entirety of our beings. It is the God of Peace Himself who sanctifies us, spirit, soul and body. He protects us from the spiritual, emotional and physical dangers we face in a fallen world. This work looks on to the coming of the Lord Jesus when we shall know salvation in all its fullness. God's work is to make us more like our Saviour, who pleased God in all the aspects of His life in this world. This morning we come to remember the Saviour who gave Himself for us and to "worship the LORD in the beauty of holiness" (Psalm 29:2). Peace reigns in our hearts as we look up to the God of Peace who has glorified the Great Shepherd of the sheep. The Holy Spirit magnifies the Lord Jesus as we bow before Him, and we are moved to live for our Saviour, spirit, soul and body.

Day 51

Monday

The God of love...peace...all grace

Finally, brethren, farewell. Become complete. Be of good comfort, be of one mind, live in peace; and the God of love and peace will be with you. (2 Corinthians 13:11)

At the end of his second letter to the Corinthian church, Paul crams some important spiritual advice into one short verse. It starts with their relationship as brothers and sisters in Christ. He bids them farewell or, as the ESV translates it, "Rejoice". Paul had to deal with some very distressing issues, but they had responded to his appeals and commands. He wanted them to ensure divisions were healed, and their fellowship restored completely. As always, he encouraged them in their Christian pathway and now urges them to be in agreement and at peace with one another. Doing these things would ensure they were in accord with the God who loved them and had given them peace. The enjoyment of the presence of the God of love and peace is dependent upon living lives which are consistent with the character of God.

The title "the God of peace" is used several times by the apostle. Paul wanted the Christians in Rome to have the experience of the God of peace being with them all (Romans 15:33). It is the privilege of Christians to be able to personally walk with God, but God also wants us to enjoy His presence, as His people. When our grandchildren were young, it was pleasant when they stayed with us one at a time. But it was also very enjoyable when they all came together and filled our house. God delights to be amongst His children and to assure them of His peace.

But we need to understand that the God of peace is the God of power. Paul writes, "And the God of peace will crush Satan under your feet shortly. The grace of our Lord Jesus Christ be with you. Amen" (Romans 16:20). At the birth of Jesus, the angels spoke of peace on earth. But bringing peace was a supreme act of power. It was the power which also abolished death and crushed Satan. God is on our side, and He still acts to defeat evil and to ensure we are not overcome by it. But to know that power we have to follow the example of the apostles. Paul encouraged the Philippians to do the things which they had seen in him. He experienced the constant presence of the God of peace and promisesd the Philippian Christians the same experience: "the God of peace will be with you" (Philippians 4:9). The power of the God of peace is gloriously seen in the resurrection of the Lord Jesus: "the God of peace who brought up our Lord Jesus from the dead, that great Shepherd of the sheep" (Hebrews 13:20). To know the God of peace is to know the power of God.

Finally, we learn of "the God of all grace, who called us to His eternal glory by Christ Jesus, after you have suffered a while, perfect, establish, strengthen, and settle you" (1 Peter 5:10). If ever there was a man who could write about the God of all grace, it was Peter. Grace transformed him. He knew there was nothing in him that deserved God's goodness, and he was fully aware of his frailties. But he had suffered, been shaped, established, strengthened and settled by the grace of God. Stephen lived in the light of the God of Glory. Peter lived in the light of the God of all Grace. That is why his last words to us were "grow in the grace and knowledge of our Lord and Saviour Jesus Christ. To Him be the glory both now and forever. Amen" (2 Peter 3:18). May we grow in grace, until by grace we are transported to glory.

Day 52

Tuesday

God has chosen the weak things

God has chosen the weak things of the world to put to shame the things which are mighty. (1 Corinthians 1:27)

The book "The London Sparrow" is about the housemaid Gladys Aylward who became a missionary in China. She failed her introductory course in preparation for full training for the mission field. Her hopes were dashed. But she was convinced God had called her to China. She spent all her savings and travelled alone on the Trans-Siberian Railway to present herself to the mission in China. The story of that journey is a remarkable story in itself of faith, determination and courage. She worked in China throughout the Second World War. During this time she recalled when the Japanese bombed the area where she lived. After a long and exhausting day helping people in her battered and frightened community, she walked wearily home. Coming to the street where her house was, she saw it was destroyed, only one wall still standing. She fell to her knees and wept uncontrollably. She was physically, emotionally and spiritually drained. When she had composed herself, she noticed a card attached to the wall of her house, blowing in the wind. She went across to read it: "God has chosen the weak things of the world to put to shame the things which are mighty" (1 Corinthians 1:27). Her tears were no longer tears of distress, but of the joy of knowing the Lord was with her in her pain.

There are times in our lives when we are overwhelmed by circumstances. We feel we have given all that we can; then one more event engulfs us. These circumstances are real, they challenge our faith, and we struggle to understand them. We are living in the present time in a crisis that has confounded the whole world. We sense the reality of our weakness.

How does God express His heart towards us? He does it through the Person of the Lord Jesus Christ. His love and grace are seen in the glory of His lowliness and His journey into our circumstances. Paul writes that we know "the grace of our Lord Jesus Christ, that though He was rich, yet for your sakes He became poor, that you through His poverty might become rich" (2 Corinthians 8:9). In this verse, Paul gives the Lord Jesus His full title, reminding us of His Person and His power. But then in the most compelling way, he reminds us of the poverty through which His Person and power are known. He became weak – "I thirst" – so that He could demonstrate the power of His love – "It is finished".

During the same world war in London, a pregnant young woman stood beside her bombed home in the city. Like Gladys Aylward, she was overcome by distress. A lady came alongside her to try and comfort her. After a little while, a man approached to explain that it was time to go. As the lady said goodbye, the young woman realised her comforter was the Queen, the mother of our present Queen. We cannot always explain our circumstances. But we can experience the presence of the Lord through His word, His abiding Holy Spirit and our brothers and sisters in the fellowship of life, which is His Church. Tears and pain are real, and so are faith and hope. Tears will be wiped away, and one day there will be no more pain. Faith and hope will be fulfilled by God's eternal love that does not fail.

Day 53

Wednesday

Intergenerational togetherness: Abraham and Isaac

So the two of them went together.   *(Genesis 22:8)*

I was asked recently to speak on the subject of intergenerational togetherness, based on the relationship between Abraham and Isaac. I must confess to initially finding the title, the topic and the characters challenging. I discovered that Abraham and Isaac are the first of many examples of intergenerational togetherness throughout the Bible. So what is this subject all about? It's about the spiritual relationship between the people of God across different generations. Sometimes, like Abraham and Isaac, it's about a father and son relationship, but this is not always the case. What it does involve is mutual love and respect, and spiritual harmony between older and younger people.

We see this harmony between Abraham and Isaac in one of the most powerful incidents in the whole of the Bible. Spiritual relationships begin with God. God says to Abraham, "Take now your son, your only *son* Isaac, whom you love, and go to the land of Moriah, and offer him there as a burnt offering on one of the mountains of which I shall tell you" (v. 2). Abraham had never been afraid of questioning God, and God had taught His friend to trust him completely. Abraham didn't speak; he simply went in complete faith and obedience to Moriah. In doing so, he teaches us not only to have a living faith, but to share that faith with the next generation, in his case Isaac and the young servants. You might be thinking, "But wasn't God destroying the next generation?" But then you would be travelling too quickly in your thoughts.

When Abraham gets close to the place of sacrifice, he says to his servants, "Stay here with the donkey; the lad and I will go yonder and worship, and we will come back to you." The man of God demonstrates his absolute faith in God by assuring the servants and Isaac he would return with his son. As they continue the last part of the journey, Isaac asks his father, "Where is the lamb for a burnt offering?" and Abraham gives the answer, "My son, God will provide for Himself the lamb for a burnt offering" (vv. 6-8). And they went on together. When they arrived, Abraham built and prepared an altar and laid Isaac on it. It was difficult, if not impossible, naturally speaking, for Abraham, an old man, to force Isaac, a young man, to lie on the altar. The impression we are given is that Isaac did so willingly. When God intervenes, we understand that He is proving Abraham's faith in circumstances which also stimulated the faith of Isaac. The father and son both trusted in the living God. And God provided a substitute, the ram. Thus, not only would they return, but God had provided a sacrifice.

I think that at Moriah, God, at the beginning of the Bible, was teaching us about something which would happen centuries later: when God the Father and God the Son would walk in harmony in this world, and when the Son would lay down His life as the great Substitute and Saviour of the world. God does not always take us to the place of sacrifice to actually make a sacrifice, but to show us His heart. The experiences of the journey of faith are experiences which He wants us to share with the next generation so that the faith of both are enriched and blessed. This living faith is expressed in a fellowship of life in which we should always value one another.

Day 54

Thursday

The Lord's Prayer: worshipping, seeking, and thankful hearts

"Our Father in heaven, hallowed be Your name. Your kingdom come." *(Luke 11:1)*

The Lord gives us what has become known as the Lord's Prayer in Luke 11:2-4 and Matthew 6:9-13. It begins with worship: "Our Father in heaven, hallowed be Your name" (Luke 11:1). In these opening words, we have God's person, God's home, and God's name brought before us. The prayer teaches us that we have a relationship with God as our Father. It is a relationship of nearness, but there is also a sense of God's greatness and holiness. We should never take God for granted or cease to be reverent in His presence.

There is also an understanding of where God is – in heaven. Prayer is a powerful link between earth and heaven. Even in today's world, with its bewildering range of technology, sometimes communications break down. Mobile phones are not always answered. The Internet can lose its connection. But we never lose our connection with God. He is always there to listen and respond to our prayers:

"For the eyes of the LORD are on the righteous,
And His ears are open to their prayers" (1 Peter 3:12).

The Lord's Prayer expresses a desire for God's kingdom to come. At the Lord's Supper, we remember His death in the light of His return. We can also pray for our present needs, being mindful of Christ's return and the fulfilment of all God's purposes in this world and in eternity. God will be glorified in the future, and it is our desire that He should be glorified in our lives now.

The Lord's Prayer then turns to God's will: "Your will be done, on earth as it is in heaven." This is a vital part of the Lord's Prayer. In the Garden of Gethsemane, Jesus prayed for the Father's will to be done. The will of God is central to our prayers. We don't pray for our will to be fulfilled, but to know, and seek to do, God's will in our lives. At a personal level, much of God's will is simple to understand. The attributes of the fruit of the Spirit in Galatians 5 and those of the love of God in 1 Corinthians 13 are the features God wants to see in us. We need grace to manifest these things. Other aspects of God's will, for example who we marry or which career we take up, need to be brought to the throne of grace for wise decisions to be made. And we should pray for others to know the mind and will of God.

The Lord Jesus' prayer then turns to our daily needs. We recognise all our blessings come from the heart and hand of God (James 1:17). This makes us a thankful people. There was once a Christian farmer who was invited to an important banquet. Alongside him were some well-educated but rude guests. At the beginning of the banquet, the farmer bowed his head and gave thanks for the meal. One of the guests scornfully asked the farmer if everyone down on the farm gave thanks for their food. "No," replied the farmer, "the animals never give thanks!" Paul reminded the Colossians, "And let the peace of God rule in your hearts, to which also you were called in one body; and be thankful" (Colossians 3:15). Our prayers should always express thankfulness. "Be anxious for nothing, but in everything by prayer and supplication, with thanksgiving, let your requests be made known to God" (Philippians 4:6).

Day 55

Friday

The Lord's Prayer: forgiving and protected hearts

*"And do not lead us into temptation,
But deliver us from the evil one."* (Luke 11:4)

Willingness to forgive is the next aspect of the Lord's Prayer. The Lord Jesus teaches us to confess our sins and also to be willing to forgive others, thereby displaying the character of God revealed in Christ: "Bearing with one another, and forgiving one another, if anyone has a complaint against another; even as Christ forgave you, so you also must do" (Colossians 3:13). This is not an easy process. We can be deeply hurt by the things we suffer from others. But forgiveness sets us free from bitterness and leaves our pain in the hands of God. It reminds us, too, that we can also hurt others and should put things right.

Prayer for God's protection for ourselves and others from temptation and evil is essential. We are all capable of making the most dreadful mistakes and we live in a world where temptation abounds. The Lord told Peter, James and John to "watch and pray, lest you enter into temptation" (Matthew 26:41). Peter later writes, "Therefore be serious and watchful in your prayers" (1 Peter 4:7). We should always be alert to spiritual dangers and not sleepwalk into situations which will harm ourselves and others. We are rarely caught out by the obvious, but more likely to be drawn away by what seems unharmful. Each day June and I pray that God will go before us, guiding our steps and keeping us close to the Saviour, never forgetting that, as He prayed for Peter so long ago, He has each of us in His heart.

We used to live near Oldham in Lancashire, which was once Winston Churchill's constituency. One day, when he was campaigning in an election, Churchill asked a passer-by if he would vote for him. "Vote for you!" exclaimed the man, "I would rather vote for the devil." To which Churchill replied, "As far as I know, the devil is not standing in this election, so perhaps you might vote for me!" Too often we can unintentionally "vote for the devil" by giving way to temptation. Prayer keeps us from the evil one and away from spiritual and moral dangers.

Prayer was a vital part of the Lord's ministry. It has always impressed me that the disciples' desire to pray effectively came from witnessing this ministry. One disciple asked the Lord, "Teach us to pray." The fact the "The Lord's Prayer" can be repeated without thought should not prevent us from seriously considering its themes. Our prayers should lift our spirits to God, our Father, in worship. His will should be our primary concern. John reminds us, "If we confess our sins, He is faithful and just to forgive us our sins and to cleanse us from all unrighteousness." We experience the forgiveness of God, and, in forgiving others, we express the heart of God. The Lord Jesus also teaches us the importance of asking that we should live holy lives. Before going to the cross, Jesus prayed, "I do not pray that You should take them out of the world, but that You should keep them from the evil one" (John 17:15). He added afterwards, "I also have sent them into the world." God's answers to the themes of the Lord's Prayer enable us to abide in Christ and "to walk just as He walked" and to witness to the glory of His grace in this world (1 John 2:6).

Day 56

Saturday

Ceaseless prayer

Pray without ceasing   *(1 Thessalonians 5:17)*

Ceaseless prayer is characterised by faith. The Lord Jesus teaches us to "ask in prayer, believing" (Matthew 21:22) and the Epistle to the Hebrews explains, "But without faith it is impossible to please Him, for he who comes to God must believe that He is, and that He is a rewarder of those who diligently seek Him" (Hebrews 11:6). This principle of prayer has not changed. It has been said that prayer is the key to heaven, and faith is the hand that turns that key.

Ceaseless prayer is characterised by patience. Jesus tells the story of the widow in Luke 18:1-8, who persistently pleaded for justice from an unjust judge until he answered her cry. Patience is a characteristic of the Christian life and one which we learn through a patient prayer life. God teaches us to await His time and discover that His timing is always perfect.

Ceaseless prayer is characterised by righteousness. James also writes about prayer and uses the example of Elijah, "The effectual fervent prayer of a righteous man availeth much" (James 5:16, AV). James teaches us that to be effective in prayer we have to live lives consistent with the will of God, that is, righteous lives. It is no use expecting God to answer our prayers if we are not following Christ. It is no use speaking about the love of God if I refuse to forgive. It is no use talking about the holiness of God if I am dishonest.

Ceaseless prayer is characterised by fervency. Elijah lived righteously and prayed fervently. To him, praying was a strenuous, not a passive, activity. It needed effort. It is a measurement of how deeply we feel about the matters God lays on our hearts. He wants us to reach out to Him and prove His ability to bless. This takes time and effort, but if we are to know God's power, we need to make this sacrifice.

Ceaseless prayer is characterised by clarity. We can develop prayer jargon and lose clarity in speaking to God. Need clarifies our prayers. Peter cried, "Lord, save me." It is having the sense in our hearts, as we come to the Throne of Grace, that it is the only place where our needs can be met. The Lord Jesus encourages us to pray succinctly, "And when you pray, do not use vain repetitions as the heathen do. For they think that they will be heard for their many words" (Matthew 6:7). Our private prayer and our prayer meetings should be filled with a spiritual focus and the consciousness of God's willingness to answer our appeals, through grace. They should also be places where we clearly express our thankfulness and worship.

If I were to shoot an arrow at the moon, the further it travelled the weaker its force would become, and eventually it would fall to the ground, never reaching its target. When we look up to heaven and pray, we are very conscious of our weakness, but the intercession of the Holy Spirit and of our blessed Saviour ensures our prayers do not limp to the Throne of Grace but arrive in power. As we begin another week, worshipping our Saviour in glory, may we, in ceaseless prayer, continue to look up to Him "at the right hand of God, who also makes intercession for us" (Romans 8:34).

Day 57

Sunday

A broken heart that re-built a city

"Why should my face not be sad, when the city, the place of my fathers' tombs lies waste, and its gates are burned with fire?"

(Nehemiah 2:3)

I have always found so much spiritual help in the books of Ezra, Nehemiah and Esther. They begin in places of desolation and darkness and end in remarkable blessing. God had to humble His people and take them to the lowest place so that He could teach them His faithfulness and power. The people we meet in these books were godly people who suffered because their nation had turned its back on God. They went into exile and experienced the bitterness of being robbed of all they held precious. Yet in a foreign land and a culture of idolatry, they maintained a living faith in a living God.

But the return to Jerusalem to build the temple did not begin in the hearts of godly Jews. It began in the heart of God. In the opening verse of the book of Ezra we read: "Now in the first year of Cyrus king of Persia, that the word of the LORD by the mouth of Jeremiah might be fulfilled, the LORD stirred up the spirit of Cyrus king of Persia" (Ezra 1:1). The monarch was commanded directly by God to rebuild the temple and a remnant of people returned to Judah, and there we learn of the ministry of Ezra. Some 20 years later, Nehemiah heard about the walls of Jerusalem being in ruins and it broke his heart, "So it was, when I heard these words, that I sat down and wept, and mourned for many days; I was fasting and praying before the God of heaven" (Nehemiah 1:4).

There are many things which can break our hearts and fill them with a sense of hopelessness. We can be trapped by wounds that will not heal and pain that will not go away. Nehemiah's broken-heartedness took him into the presence of God. Day after day he allowed his tears to flow and grief to overwhelm him. He pleaded with God in prayer, confessing his people's sin, and appealed to Him to restore them. And he asked God to grant him mercy in the sight of the king. But unlike Hannah, who prayed and then was no longer sad, Nehemiah's sadness could not be hidden, and it put his life at risk. He served a monarch who held supreme power, who could end a servant's life without a second thought. And the king recognised Nehemiah's "sorrow of heart".

It is astonishing that the empire that destroyed Jerusalem and made its people captive was succeeded by another empire whose monarch God instructed to rebuild the temple. Then years later, He used Nehemiah's broken heart to influence King Artaxerxes to allow him to rebuild the walls of Jerusalem.

It was the Lord's broken heartedness that led to our redemption. Our broken-heartedness is not without purpose:

> The sacrifices of God are a broken spirit,
> A broken and a contrite heart
> These, O God, You will not despise (Psalm 51:17).

May we have the faith to place our sorrow in the hands of the Man of Sorrows, so that we do not sorrow, for the joy of the Lord is our strength (see Nehemiah 8:10).

Day 58

Monday

Vision

"Do not fear, for those who are with us are more than those who are with them." And Elisha prayed, and said, "LORD, I pray, open his eyes that he may see." (2 Kings 6:16-17)

A few years ago I had a problem with the small muscles around my right eye that caused double vision. This was particularly disturbing, as it occurred suddenly whilst I was driving in the Swiss Alps! It took some months to recover, during which time I could not drive. I had to face endless questions about where my parrot was and there were very poor imitations of Long John Silver. But the positive side was that it made me think about the preciousness of our sight and the things that go wrong when it is distorted. And it made me consider our spiritual vision and the problems we can face.

Here are some physical eye-problems that provide interesting illustrations of how our spiritual vision can be distorted:

Diplopia is the word for double vision. The Lord warns us that we cannot serve God and riches (Matthew 6:24) and James reminds us of the dangers of being double-minded (James 1:8).

Cataracts develop slowly. They cause cloudy vision, the fading of colours and the diminishing of sight at night. As we get older, we are more likely to suffer from these. It takes surgery to restore clear sight. Sometimes things come into our lives slowly but introduce a distance between us and the Lord. Over time this develops and the joy of our salvation is lost and the Lord has to intervene to remove what spoils our communion with Him (Revelation 2:4). Myopia is near- or short-sightedness. We cannot see distant objects clearly, only those which are close. Selfishness is something which affects us all. It makes *my* interests paramount. This can even emerge in Christian service and ministry, when we have little room for others and their contributions.

Hyperopia is far-sightedness. Distant objects are clear, but objects close to us are blurred. It is the opposite of near-sightedness. We can ignore, or count of less importance, the responsibilities we have towards people and things close to us, and become more focussed on remote things, which exclude others but satisfy our interests.

Retinitis Pigmentosa is a disease of the eye, and a cause of tunnel vision. Sufferers lose their peripheral vision. This illustrates obsessive behaviour in spiritual matters.

Glaucoma is caused by pressure and can result in the loss of sight if the pressure is not normalised. Pressure in our lives is real and can overwhelm us as we try to carry too many burdens, especially those God does not ask us to carry (1 Peter 5:7).

God wants us to have opened eyes and to see clearly by faith. Elisha prayed for his servant's eyes to be opened. By "looking unto Jesus" we bring every aspect of our lives into focus. We don't have mixed motives, our fellowship with God is not undermined, we are not limited by selfishness, we have a balanced care for those people and things which are our responsibility, we are not obsessed by secular or spiritual service, and we are able to bear one another's burdens. Seeing the Lord brings peace and power to our lives. Over the next few days I want to explore the practical application of "Looking unto Jesus", that is, what this means, and how we enjoy the clear, spiritual vision the Lord wants us to have and the benefits which come from it.

Day 59

Tuesday

Double vision

Looking unto Jesus, the author and finisher of our faith.
(Hebrews 12:2)

Prolonged double vision is an unpleasant experience. It disturbs your balance, makes simple movements difficult, and significantly reduces your ability to operate normally. This physical abnormality gives us a vivid insight into what happens if we suffer from spiritual double vision. In simple terms, it is looking at two things at once. In the physical world, we realise straight away that this is a significant problem. In my case, I had to wear a patch over my right eye to ensure I could see properly out of my left eye and keep my balance. But this is not what happens spiritually. So often we persuade ourselves that we can live in fellowship with God whilst being conformed to the world which is at enmity with God. This is not a new phenomenon. Gideon clearly illustrates this. In his day, the people of God suffered terribly at the hands of the Midianites. They prayed to the Lord for deliverance. When God called Gideon, the first thing he did was to destroy the idols in his own city. The people appealed to God for help, at the same time continuing to worship idols. After the people of God returned from exile in Babylon, they did not return to worshipping idols like Baal. But gradually other idols appeared: materialism and self-righteousness. What compounds the problem of spiritual double vision is double-mindedness. The Lord highlights the folly of this: "No one can serve two masters; for either he will hate the one and love the other, or else he will be loyal to the one and despise the other. You cannot serve God and mammon" (Matthew 6:24).

Being double-minded makes us unstable: "a double-minded man, unstable in all his ways" (James 1:8). The reason for being double-minded is a lack of faith (v. 6). James appeals to the double-minded: "Draw near to God and He will draw near to you" (James 4:8) and instructs them to confront the unholiness of their lives. By "Looking unto Jesus" we learn what we are and who He is. James saw the remedy for failure and disobedience and the power for Christian living as coming into the presence of God. In the Lord's presence, I learn to love by seeing His love. I learn compassion by seeing His compassion. I learn obedience by seeing His obedience. For our lives to be in balance with the mind and will God we must come to Him:

> I will instruct you and teach you in the way you should go;
> I will guide you with My eye (Psalm 32:8).

Once we make Christ the single object of our faith, every aspect of our lives comes into focus. "Looking unto Jesus" is not a vague thing. It brings clarity and purpose to our daily living. The Lord leads us in "paths of righteousness" and protects us.

This spiritual clarity also brings the constant challenge of faith and action. Single vision is about seeing clearly what God wants us to do, and doing it. True discipleship is about daily steps of faith. I remember once walking up a steep path with an older sister who was a great help in my life. She said, "Gordon, always take small steps when you are going uphill." She was giving me practical advice about conserving energy, but she taught me an important spiritual lesson I have never forgotten. By looking each day into the face of Jesus Christ, I am empowered to take those critical, small steps of faith and, in doing so, know that God will prepare me for the big ones.

Day 60

Wednesday

Cataracts

"Abide in Me, and I in you." (John 15:4)

Small steps of faith keep us close to God. Small steps of disobedience take us away from God. I remember at one of our young couples' weekends talking with one of them about the busyness of life. They explained how difficult it was sometimes to find time for themselves. We talked about how important it is to pause and reflect on the direction our lives are taking and to assess things together in the Lord's presence. We have to make time. Cataracts rarely appear overnight. They gradually develop. It is the same with our relationships. They can fail because distance gradually replaces nearness. And our relationship with the Lord can suffer in the same way and we lose what is most precious and most powerful.

The Ephesian church was so blessed. Paul writes with joy in his heart of their spiritual progress: "Therefore I also, after I heard of your faith in the Lord Jesus and your love for all the saints, do not cease to give thanks for you" (Ephesians 1:15-16). In the next chapter he speaks of their nearness to God through the work of Christ (v. 13). In Acts 20 he prepares the elders of the church at Ephesus for coming spiritual dangers. Never was a church so well cared for as the church at Ephesus. In Revelation 2 the Lord commends them still for their work, patience and carefulness, but then has to say, "Nevertheless I have this against you, that you have left your first love" (Revelation 2:4). Nearness had been replaced by distance. Service is never a replacement for communion. True service is the result of fellowship with Christ. The Lord gave everything to bring us near to Himself, to know His love, to abide in it and have fruitful lives. The parable of the Prodigal Son in Luke 15 teaches us that God does not move away from us but we move away from God. This problem was not only seen in the younger son who went into a far country, but it was also true of the older son who never left his father's house.

So how do we prevent things coming into our lives which blur our vision of the glory of Christ and His love for us? During lockdown I started to begin each day looking up to God with a simple prayer that He would give me an impression of the wonder of the person and work of the Lord Jesus Christ. The objectives of this prayer are that I would

- have fellowship with the Father, who said, "This is My beloved Son. Hear Him!" (Luke 9:35)

- have fellowship with the Spirit, whose ministry is to glorify the Son in our hearts (John 16:14), and

- have fellowship with the Saviour, who said, "Abide in me and I in you."

I believe this and similar prayers keep us in the love and grace of God, and protect us from the things which would distance us from Him.

The Lord says in John 15, "He who abides in Me, and I in him, bears much fruit; for without Me you can do nothing" (v. 5). The Lord's presence takes the clouds away from our eyes, and in seeing Him clearly we see everything else in our lives clearly. The Father undertakes the work of Divine Vinedresser, ensuring we become like the Saviour. And the Holy Spirit empowers us to follow Christ in energetic, joyful and sacrificial service.

Day 61

Thursday

Short-sightedness

Let each of you look out not only for his own interests but also for the interests of others. (Philippians 2:4)

Short-sightedness is when we cannot see distant objects clearly, only those which are close. It provides a helpful illustration of a spiritual problem. The church at Philippi was very dear to Paul's heart. There was ample evidence of their love for the apostle. This love was expressed in their sacrificial giving. In chapter 2, Paul presents to them most beautifully the mind of Christ. Before doing this, he encourages them not to be short-sighted by only being occupied with their own interests, but to see ways in which they could also look after the interests of others. They already had some excellent examples – Lydia and the Philippian jailer, founding members of the church at Philippi. These dear saints, so different in background, had immediately been taught by the Holy Spirit to see and minister to the needs of others in love. Now, Paul shows them the greatest example of all. He describes how Christ Jesus humbled Himself and became obedient unto death to ensure our salvation. He saw and met us in all our need.

But if you look carefully at what Paul writes, he wasn't saying you should not look after your own interests. A vital feature of the Christian life is that we do take responsibility for our own spiritual welfare. In Acts 20, Paul encourages the Ephesian elders, "Therefore take heed to yourselves and to all the flock, among which the Holy Spirit has made you overseers, to shepherd the church of God which He purchased with His own blood" (v. 28). John writes, "Look to yourselves, that we do not lose those things we worked for, but that we may receive a full reward" (2 John 1:8). We have a responsibility to ensure we are spiritually healthy; by doing so we can spiritually care for our wives, husbands, children, and brothers and sisters in Christ, and other people. God has given us a clear field of vision, embracing what is near and what is further away.

In the parable of the Good Samaritan the Lord teaches about seeing need and responding to it (Luke 10). The priest and the Levite saw the wounded man and both chose to pass by on the other side. They saw, but they did not respond. Instead, they deliberately put distance between themselves and a fellow human being in great need. They blinded themselves. The Samaritan saw the wounded man, had compassion, went to him with healing power and took care of him. In Exodus 3 the Lord spoke to Moses of the sufferings of His people, and the first thing He says is, "I have surely seen the oppression of My people who are in Egypt" (v. 7); then He promises to come down to deliver them.

As Christians we see with our human eyes and we see by faith. In both cases, God enables us to see so that we will respond. Sometimes that response is worship and at other times it is sacrificial service. God shows us in our personal lives, our families, amongst the people of God, and in the world, what needs our careful attention. He opens our eyes to the glory of the Saviour who saw our need, came down in lowly grace, and delivered us. That glory does not blind us; it opens our eyes and empowers us to act.

Day 62

Friday

Far-sightedness

And not many days after, the younger son gathered all together, journeyed to a far country …   *(Luke 15:13)*

These all died in faith, not having received the promises, but having seen them afar off were assured of them, embraced them and confessed that they were strangers and pilgrims on the earth.
(Hebrews 11:13)

Our sight is remarkable. We can see things which are near and things which are far away, and we can process what we see to co-ordinate our movements. Problems occur when our sight is limited by short-sightedness or by Hyperopia – far-sightedness. In the latter case, distant objects are clearer, but objects close to us are blurred. This is compounded by what we choose to view. And this illustrates the spiritual problem of ignoring, or counting of less importance, the responsibilities we have towards people and things close to us, and being more focussed on things which exclude others, but satisfy our interests and ambitions.

We have a vivid illustration of this in the parable of the Prodigal Son. He was far-sighted. His eyes were firmly fixed on the "far country", with all its promised freedom and excitement. His desire did not start the day before he left home. It was something he had already chosen and set his heart on long before. He could not wait to leave his father's house, because he had never understood his father's love. This love ultimately transformed the prodigal son's field of vision. We often exclusively use this parable to preach the gospel. But it teaches us deep lessons about dissatisfaction, materialism, love of the world, loss, conviction, repentance, restoration and, above all, the depth of God's love. This path of painful learning can be experienced by Christians.

Caleb was also a man who was far-sighted. As a spy in the Promised Land, he had seen the beauty of a land "flowing with milk and honey". Caleb believed that God would enable the children of Israel to possess the Promised Land. But that did not happen straight away, and he spent the next four decades waiting for that hope to be realised. But how did he live those 40 years? In bitterness and resentment? No! He followed the LORD with all his heart. He proved his faith in all the confinement and testing of the wilderness. And all the time his heart was filled with a living hope. His far-sightedness empowered his daily living. His eyes of faith looked on to the day when he would enter the Promised Land and possess Hebron (Joshua 14).

God wants us to see by faith the responsibilities and blessings of the here and now. At the same time, ahead of us, we have a living hope that empowers us to live for Him in the present. By His word being applied to our hearts through the ministry of the Holy Spirit of God, He opens our eyes to what lies ahead and gives us the vision to understand the path He wants us to take. Along the way, we will be tempted and our faith will be tested, sometimes severely. Like Demas, we can end up loving the world (2 Timothy 4:10). Like Peter, we can see the waves of uncertainty surrounding us and begin to be overwhelmed (Matthew 14:30). But we have a Saviour who has the power to save and the power to restore. Peter experienced both. And by "looking unto Jesus" day by day, He brings every aspect of our lives into perspective and teaches us to walk by faith and to please Him (Hebrews 11:6).

Day 63

Monday

Tunnel vision

Now it came to pass, when the time had come for Him to be received up, that He steadfastly set His face to go to Jerusalem.

(Luke 9:51)

Retinitis Pigmentosa is a disease of the eye and a cause of tunnel vision. Sufferers lose their peripheral vision. I remember a sister who had this problem explaining to me how it limited what she could see. She said it was just like being inside a tunnel and only seeing what was at the end.

There are times in our lives when we need to focus on one thing. Our eyes enable us to do this, just as our normal hearing has the ability to concentrate our listening. In spiritual matters we do have priorities. In our verse this morning the Lord was focussed on fulfilling the work He had come into the world to accomplish. But as He took the journey to Jerusalem He continued to act in grace and love. When the cross and all that it meant was immediately before the Lord Jesus, He still had in view the spiritual welfare of His disciples; indeed, of us all. Whilst He was being mistreated by the spiritual leaders of Israel, He was able to look at Peter. And on the cross, dying for the sin of the world, He looked upon His mother, John and a dying thief.

We can be overcome by obsessive behaviour. This can affect us in our secular responsibilities. Our careers can absorb us and take up all our energies. Interests outside of work can be equally addictive. I loved playing rugby and our school had a very successful team. Some of my friends went on to play professionally and for Great Britain. There are faithful Christians who play international sport. I had the opportunity to continue to carry on playing, but I think the Lord knew that for me it would become all-absorbing, and I gave the sport up. The Lord knows our different characters and guides us to make the decisions which are right for us.

There is also the danger that we can become obsessive in spiritual matters. Worldliness is not confined to the secular world; it is overwhelmingly evident in the religious world. The Lord Jesus took a lot of time highlighting the obsessive legalism and hypocrisy of the Pharisees, priests and Levites. He knows how religion can distort the minds and actions of people. History and present events bear testimony to this behaviour.

We need vision. We need this personally and we need it as the people of God. It is in "Looking unto Jesus" that this vision is given. Our vision should never cause us to belittle or judge others: it should energise our service and embrace fellow believers in love and understanding. The ungodly Pharisees, and they were not all ungodly people, fell victim to wanting to be seen as more holy than others. They compared themselves to others and judged themselves to be better: "The Pharisee stood and prayed thus with himself, 'God, I thank You that I am not like other men'" (Luke 18:11). Our vision should never make us think and act in this way. We are sinners saved by grace and we need that same grace to make us more like the Saviour who loves us. It is in the presence of the Saviour that our spiritual sight is balanced and focussed, and we learn to worship, work and witness with hearts ruled by the love of God.

Day 64

Sunday

They saw His glory

But Peter and those with him were heavy with sleep; and when they were fully awake, they saw His glory. (Luke 9:32)

For He received from God the Father honour and glory when such a voice came to Him from the Excellent Glory: "This is My beloved Son, in whom I am well pleased." And we heard this voice which came from heaven when we were with Him on the holy mountain. (2 Peter 1:17-18)

As Peter comes to the end of his life, we see His closeness to the Lord. He had learnt so much as he humbly followed the Saviour in faith. The Gospels record the brightness of his faith, alongside his mistakes and failures. But ultimately his life was a triumph of grace, characterised by those simple final words of the Lord to him, "You follow me" (John 21:22). Grace transformed Peter into a true shepherd who cared for the Flock of God. His final words to us at the end of this book are, "but grow in the grace and knowledge of our Lord and Saviour Jesus Christ. To Him be the glory both now and forever. Amen" (2 Peter 3:18).

Peter understood the power of grace. Grace saves us, and by it, we grow in the knowledge of Christ as our Lord and as our Saviour. On a rooftop in Joppa, in Acts 10, Peter said to the Lord, "Not so Lord" (v. 14). My father often used to say to me, "Don't contradict!" It took some time for Peter to learn this lesson, and his contradictions led him into very deep waters. It was the grace of God to the Gentiles, that retaught him not to contradict, but to live in humility and simple obedience to the Lord who loved him, and that love extended to everyone.

Peter also wanted us to grow in the knowledge of Jesus as the Saviour. When we think of the Saviour, we tend to look backwards. But the Lord never ceases to be our Saviour. We well know He saves us from the penalty, the power and the presence of sin, and we need to live in the reality of these truths.

Peter ends with the glory of the Lord: at the end of his life, he recounts the Father's delight in His Son. In the first chapter of his second letter he relates the occasion when he, James and John were with the Lord on the Mount of Transfiguration and "they saw His glory" (Luke 9:32): he remembers that he and his friends "were with Him on the holy mountain".

When we remember the Lord, by faith, we see the glory of His deity, His manhood, His ministry, His sufferings and His death. We also see the glory of His resurrection and ascension. By faith we see Him now crowned with glory and honour. And in hope, we look on to His millennial glory, and His glory in the eternal day. In this way, we respond in the power of the Spirit in worship. By remembering Christ's love, we are reminded of the day when we shall be with Him to behold His glory: "Father, I desire that they also whom You gave Me may be with Me where I am, that they may behold My glory which You have given Me; for You loved Me before the foundation of the world" (John 17:24).

Day 65

Monday

Pressured vision

"Teacher, do You not care that we are perishing?"   *(Mark 4:38).*

Every morning I put an eye-drop in each of my eyes. In the evening I repeat this and put an additional drop in my left eye. This is to control the pressure in my eyes, because I suffer from Glaucoma. Increased pressure in the eyes can result in the loss of sight. My eye-drops keep the pressure normalised.

Pressure in our lives is real. Sometimes this pressure comes from a single source, like illness, redundancy, or COVID-19. But often it is a combination of things: the "many things" Jesus spoke to Martha about in Luke 10:41. We are also different in character. Some of us are quickly stressed, and others absorb and even thrive on pressure.

Pressure builds up until something within us breaks down. The disciples experienced this: "But He (Jesus) was in the stern, asleep on a pillow. And they awoke Him and said to Him, 'Teacher, do You not care that we are perishing?'" This was a critical moment in their relationship with the Lord. The Lord was asleep, but present. He was demonstrating, through His lowliness as a man, the power that never ceased to be His. The disciples believed the Lord could help them, but He needed to be awake. Did they think that, if the Lord had not woken up, they would have perished? In the event, they had the remarkable experience of witnessing the Lord's power to remove all danger in an instant. But afterwards the Lord said to them, "Why are you so fearful? How is it that you have no faith?" (v. 40). The Lord was indicating that, whilst He was with them, they were safe. He was not disturbed by the storm. But He was concerned that His disciples did not trust Him, nor experienced the love that casts out fear. They feared the storm and doubted His care when He wanted them to know His peace and keeping power in the midst of the greatest pressure.

In Acts 12 Peter was right at the centre of another storm – Herod's persecution of the Church. He was arrested, imprisoned and was awaiting execution. What did he do in such a desperate situation? He fell sound asleep! How? Because he knew the Lord was with him. Although Stephen was not spared a cruel death, his experience also teaches us that he knew the Lord was with him, and he fell asleep in Jesus (Acts 7:60).

The Lord may not always take us out of our circumstances. This does not mean He does not care. He always wants us to know His presence in the pressures of life. These experiences are intended to form His likeness in us. If pressure engulfs us, and it can, we find peace in casting all our cares upon Him (1 Peter 5:7). "Casting" is the action of throwing a covering on the back of a colt (Luke 19:35). Our salvation is described by the Lord's illustration of a shepherd placing the lost sheep on His shoulders (Luke 15:5). Isaiah 50:6 speaks prophetically of the Lord Jesus, "I gave My back to those who struck Me." The Lord carries us in the power of His redeeming love that was stronger than death. There is no better place to be when we are facing life's many pressures than in the Lord's presence. There we find all our answers. Like my eye-drops, each day we need to apply the word of God to our hearts and be assured by the One who said, "I will never leave you nor forsake you" (Hebrews 13:5).

Day 66

Tuesday

Shadrach, Meshach, Abed-Nego and Immanuel

"Look!" he answered, "I see four men loose, walking in the midst of the fire; and they are not hurt, and the form of the fourth is like the Son of God." (Daniel 3:25)

There are passages in the Bible where faith leaps out in the midst of conflict and shines with a brightness that lifts our souls, and encourages us to follow the Lord in living faith. What is also uplifting is that Shadrach, Meshach and Abed-Nego had a fellowship of faith. We should never lose sight of the importance of Christian friendship. It is important to have friends we can trust and who trust us. Friends who are close enough to both encourage and rebuke. Friends who deepen our faith in God.

In chapter 2, Daniel and his three friends were in danger of being slaughtered by a powerful and unreasonable monarch. King Nebuchadnezzar had lost his temper with his advisors because they could not tell him his dream and interpret it. It was Daniel's bravery in asking the king for more time which saved many lives. Then Daniel held in his house what has been described as the first recording in the Bible of a prayer meeting (2:17-19). Daniel and his three friends prayed, and God revealed Nebuchadnezzar's dream to Daniel and explained its meaning. Daniel was a man of extraordinary faith, but he also greatly valued his spiritual friends. May the present crisis stimulate us to cultivate a fellowship of prayer.

But although the dream revealed that Nebuchadnezzar's empire was under the authority of the God of heaven (2:37), he still erects a golden image. Worst still, he made it law that everyone should worship it. Soon it came to light that Shadrach, Meshach and Abed-Nego were not obeying the king's command and were summoned into his presence. He gave them a final opportunity to bow down to his idol or face death. It is at this point we see their glorious faith. These three exiled friends, enslaved in a world they did not belong to, were confronted by a furious king with enormous power. They did not hesitate for a moment to express their complete faith in God: "Our God whom we serve is able to deliver us from the burning fiery furnace, and He will deliver us from your hand, O king. But if not, let it be known to you, O king, that we do not serve your gods, nor will we worship the gold image which you have set up" (Daniel 3:17-18). And they were cast into a furnace of fire.

What happens next illustrates the keeping power of God. The fire did not harm them in any way. They walked amongst the flames but were not alone. There was a fourth Person whose glory the Babylonians found difficult to describe, one like the Son of God. Shadrach, Meshach and Abed-Nego's experience demonstrates the Lord's deliverance in a way we should never forget. In the Old Testament, God constantly and in numerous ways delivered His people by taking them out of dangerous places. But He did not remove Shadrach, Meshach and Abed-Nego from the furnace: He went into the flames. Only when we come to the New Testament do we fully understand Immanuel, "God with us". He enters the world to save and make us His children. And He is still Immanuel. He continues to reveal Himself, not only by delivering us from fiery trials, but by walking with us amongst the flames and proving the genuineness of our faith:

"In this you greatly rejoice, though now for a little while, if need be, you have been grieved by various trials, that the genuineness of your faith, being much more precious than gold that perishes, though it is tested by fire, may be found to praise, honour, and glory at the revelation of Jesus Christ" (1 Peter 1:6-7).

Day 67

Wednesday

My church

"On this rock I will build My church, and the gates of Hades shall not prevail against it." (Matthew 16:18)

At Caesarea Philippi, Jesus asked His disciples a vital question, "Who do men say that I, the Son of Man, am?" They said, "Some say John the Baptist, some Elijah, and others Jeremiah or one of the prophets." Then He asked them, "But who do you say that I am?" Simon Peter answered, "You are the Christ, the Son of the living God." In response, Jesus said to Peter, "Blessed are you, Simon Bar-Jonah, for flesh and blood has not revealed this to you, but My Father who is in heaven. And I also say to you that you are Peter, and on this rock I will build My church, and the gates of Hades shall not prevail against it" (Matthew 16:13-18).

Jesus promises to build His Church, and He is the person on whom it is built. He is the chief cornerstone (Ephesians 2:20). The cornerstone (or foundation stone) was the first stone laid, and it determined the vertical and horizontal aspects of the entire building. All other stones were placed in reference to this one great stone. As Peter describes in 1 Peter 2:4, we come to Christ, to be built upon Him as the living cornerstone. He was rejected by men, but chosen by God and precious.

We read in 1 Kings 6:7 about Solomon's temple: "And the temple, when it was being built, was built with stone finished at the quarry, so that no hammer or chisel or any iron tool was heard in the temple while it was being built." This is a remarkable illustration in two ways: Christ died at Calvary, and afterwards we read, "When Joseph had taken the body, he wrapped it in a clean linen cloth, and laid it in his new tomb which he had hewn out of the rock; and he rolled a large stone against the door of the tomb…" (Matthew 27:59-60). Out of a tomb of newly hewn rock, Jesus emerges in the power of His resurrection as the living cornerstone of His soon-to-be-built Church. Also, the process of shaping temple rocks before they were put into the building is an illustration of God's work in us. We fit perfectly into Christ's glorious Church: "Coming to Him as to a living stone, rejected indeed by men, but chosen by God and precious, you also, as living stones, are being built up a spiritual house, a holy priesthood, to offer up spiritual sacrifices acceptable to God through Jesus Christ" (1 Peter 2:4-5). There is nothing more inanimate than a stone – and we are described as living stones. It is a powerful description of how we were taken out of death and made alive, possessing glorious life in our Living Head (Ephesians 2:1-10).

Christ loves each and every one of His people. And He loves the Church into which we are formed. The two words "My church" convey the depth of that love. He teaches us this in the short and simple parable of the merchant seeking beautiful pearls, "who, when he had found one pearl of great price, went and sold all that he had and bought it" (Matthew 13:46). It is this wonderful love we now, as a holy priesthood, remember this new morning. And we express our love for the Saviour, "Though you have not seen him, you love him; and even though you do not see him now, you believe in him and are filled with an inexpressible and glorious joy" (1 Peter 1:8, NIV). May His love empower us to live for Him every day.

Day 68

Thursday

Facing the uncertainty of the world in the certainty of Christ's love

"These things I have spoken to you, that in Me you may have peace. In the world you will have tribulation; but be of good cheer, I have overcome the world." (John 16: 33)

It is the apostle John who unfolds to us in considerable detail what Jesus said to His disciples as Calvary approached. He prepared them for new circumstances. We face worldwide uncertainty. In such circumstances it is good to reflect on what the Lord brought before the hearts of His disciples as uncertain times confronted them. They were in His heart.

In chapter 13 we read: "Jesus, knowing that the Father had given all things into His hands, and that He had come from God and was going to God, rose from supper and laid aside His garments, took a towel and girded Himself. After that, He poured water into a basin and began to wash the disciples' feet, and to wipe them with the towel with which He was girded" (vv. 3-5). These verses start with the glory of Christ's deity and flow seamlessly into His glory as the servant of God in this world. The love of Christ is expressed in His humility. He teaches us to serve one another in love.

The Lord opens chapter 14 with the words, "Let not your heart be troubled; you believe in God, believe also in Me" (v. 1). He presents Himself as the object of our faith. The love of Christ sustains our faith in Him, even when, like the man in Mark 9:24 who sensed the weakness of His faith, we cry out with tears, "Lord, we believe; help our unbelief!"

In Chapter 15 we see that the love of Christ stimulates us to be fruitful: "If you abide in Me, and My words abide in you, you will ask what you desire, and it shall be done for you. By this My Father is glorified, that you bear much fruit; so you will be My disciples" (vv. 7-8). His love keeps us close. The nearness we experience by abiding in Christ produces His likeness in us.

The Lord also wants us to enjoy His peace in a troubled world. In chapter 16 He says, "These things I have spoken to you, that in Me you may have peace. In the world you will have tribulation; but be of good cheer, I have overcome the world" (v. 33). Our peace is in Him, and the love of Christ gives us the strength to follow the Saviour, not simply enduring circumstances, but victoriously overcoming them.

In Chapter 17 the Son prays, "Father, I desire that they also whom You gave Me may be with Me where I am, that they may behold My glory which You have given Me; for You loved Me before the foundation of the world" (v. 24). In prayer, the Lord looked to the future when His love is satisfied, because we are with Him in glory. That day has not yet come. But the love that will take us into that eternal day already rests upon us. And, as we face uncertain times, it is the certainty of Christ's love for us that guides our path. It enables us to serve in humility, it sustains our faith in Christ, it stimulates our fruitfulness, strengthens our discipleship and secures our hope. The flame of Christ's love could not be quenched by the sufferings of Calvary. Now the victory of His love is to be seen in our lives.

Day 69

Friday

Seek those things above

If then you were raised with Christ, seek those things which are above, where Christ is, sitting at the right hand of God. Set your mind on things above, not on things on the earth. For you died, and your life is hidden with Christ in God. When Christ who is our life appears, then you also will appear with Him in glory.

(Colossians 3:1-4)

We were visiting a meeting once, and I was asked to preach the gospel. I began by saying how nice it was to be back in Keswick. A friend at the back of the hall shouted out, "Gordon, you're in Alnwick!" Alnwick is a lovely town in Northumberland, about 120 miles from Keswick (which is in the Lake District), so I was not too far off! It reminded me of being invited once to take a Sunday School prize-giving in Bradford. We arrived in plenty of time, but the hall was in complete darkness. We were confused, when it suddenly dawned on me the prize-giving was in Leeds!! It is surprising how fast you can travel from Bradford to Leeds when you set your mind to it! June tells me I make mistakes because I am thinking about one thing while doing something else.

Paul had a clear spiritual mind. He encouraged the Colossians to "seek those things which are above" and to "set (their) minds on things above". He reminds them that they are raised with Christ. This is a difficult concept. Here we are on earth, living in a material world, but Paul is saying we are raised with Christ, who is at God's right hand. He goes further by saying our lives are hidden with Christ in God. Paul explains we possess life in

Christ now and live in the good of it by faith. One day we shall experience its fulness when we "appear with Him in glory".

But Paul is also explaining that the life we have in Christ in heaven now is the power which enables us to live life abundantly on earth. You only have to look at the example of the first century Christians, and the Christian faith's rapid expansion, to see lives moved so powerfully by Christ from heaven through the Holy Spirit. Paul was a living testimony to this reality. We were thinking on Christmas Day morning about how God moved earth and heaven in reference to His Son. One day He will move His entire creation to own Jesus as Lord, to the glory of God the Father (Philippians 2:9-11). But right now He is still moving the hearts and lives of His children in this world. Through their faith, faithfulness and fruitfulness, they endeavour to live for God. And how does this happen? By setting our minds on the things above.

The Lord Jesus told us, "Seek first the kingdom of God and His righteousness, and all these things shall be added to you. Therefore do not worry about tomorrow, for tomorrow will worry about its own things. Sufficient for the day is its own trouble" (Matthew 6:33-34). The beginning of a new year is not a time for resolutions but to rely on the Lord's promise:

> I will instruct you and teach you in the way you should go;
> I will guide you with My eye (Psalm 32:8).

To be guided by His eye, we have to look into His face.

Day 70

Saturday

It is written

---

*"It is written, 'Man shall not live by bread alone, but by every word that proceeds from the mouth of God'... It is written again, 'You shall not tempt the L*ORD* your God'... It is written, 'You shall worship the L*ORD* your God, and Him only you shall serve'."*
(Matthew 4:4,7,10)

And beginning at Moses and all the Prophets, He expounded to them in all the Scriptures the things concerning Himself... "All things must be fulfilled which were written in the Law of Moses and the Prophets and the Psalms concerning Me."
(Luke 24:27,44)

The Lord begins His ministry on earth by demonstrating how vital the word of God is to the life of faith. After His baptism, Jesus is confronted by Satan. The Lord demonstrated over and over again His power over Satan through His words and His miracles. But He begins this ministry repelling his attacks with the word of God.

The Lord was showing us how important it is to live in the light of God's word. Paul writes later in the New Testament, "All Scripture is given by inspiration of God, and is profitable for doctrine, for reproof, for correction, for instruction in righteousness, that the man of God may be complete, thoroughly equipped for every good work" (2 Timothy 3:16-17). It is our guide, and through it we live holy lives: "Sanctify them by Your truth. Your word is truth" (John 17:17). God's word is never to be misused. We don't take it up to justify our own will. It shows us God's will and leads us to worship and serve Him.

In Luke's Gospel, at the end of His ministry, Jesus reveals Himself in the Old Testament Scriptures. The Lord speaks personally to two disciples on the road to Emmaus. Their hearts were moved as He expounded the Scriptures to reveal Himself. Exposition of the Scriptures should never be cold or dry. It should always move our hearts and empower us to live for Christ. The disciples then travelled to Jerusalem to share their experience of the Saviour with their fellow disciples. The Lord appears and expounds everything concerning Himself in the Old Testament.

God's word is constantly under attack and its life-blessing principles are being abandoned. In the midst of all God's blessings in Eden, Satan's route into Eve's heart was a simple question, "Has God indeed said...?" (Genesis 3:1). As the Lord experienced hunger, thirst and isolation in the wilderness, as He would at Calvary, He give us the answer, "Yes!" Scripture manifests the heart and mind of God to our hearts and minds. The disciples' hearts burned, and their understanding was opened. Through the word of God, Christ's love fills our hearts, and we are taught the mind of Christ. It is essential to the Christian experience that we open our Bibles in faith each day and seek the presence of God. In God's presence His word guides our paths, reveals His will, and enables us to worship and serve the Saviour. He shows us that His word needs to be central to our hearts, homes, fellowship and witness. In the pages of our Bibles we see our Saviour. By seeing Jesus, we learn to walk with Him and experience His sustaining power in all circumstances.

Day 71

Sunday

Stay here and watch with Me

Then He said to them, "My soul is exceedingly sorrowful, even to death. Stay here and watch with Me." (Matthew 26:38)

In the Garden of Gethsemane (Matthew 26:36-46) Peter, James and John did not see the Lord Jesus in His glory as they had on the Mount of Transfiguration. But they did hear His voice, "My soul is exceedingly sorrowful, even to death. Stay here and watch with Me." They were present when the weight of the cross bore down on His holy soul.

We see Peter, James and John being taken for the last time by the Lord into His presence as witnesses. The Lord had taken them into a home to witness His power over death. Then He took them up a mountain to see His glory. Now we see them brought into a garden to witness His suffering love. Communion with Christ is not primarily about us wanting to be in the Lord's presence, but understanding that He wants us to be in His company. In the Garden of Gethsemane, we begin to discover how much it cost the Lord to remove all the distance created by sin and disobedience. Gethsemane takes us back to Eden and to a glorious garden made as a place where God could be close to our first parents. But that garden of nearness became the place where terrible distance, with all its consequences, entered.

The Lord began His ministry in the isolation of a desert where he defeated Satan. At the close of His ministry, He measures sin's distance in a garden as He faced the isolation of Calvary. He appeals to His disciples with the words, "Stay here and watch with Me." It is humbling to know that the Lord wanted the presence of His disciples. Peter was so confident of his ability to stand by the Lord, but with James and John, and not for the first time, he fell asleep. It is to Peter that the Lord says with sadness, "What! Could you not watch with Me one hour? Watch and pray, lest you enter into temptation. The spirit indeed is willing, but the flesh is flesh is weak" (vv. 40-41). In Gethsemane, we learn our weakness, but we also witness the power of Christ's love to His Father and for us. Angels ministered at the Lord's birth, and in the desert; Luke records the ministry of an angel to the Saviour in the garden (Luke 22:43). At his birth angels rejoiced and shepherds came. In Gethsemane those He loved were there and heaven rendered angelic service. At Calvary He was alone.

In these holy moments, we learn something of the extent of the cost of our salvation and the depth of the love of the Son of God, who said to His Father, "Thy will be done" (v. 42, AV). It is our privilege to come this morning, at His invitation, to stay and look back, with worshipping hearts, to Calvary. And to trace the love that was stronger than death, and seek to respond in boundless gratitude:

> O come my soul, and gaze
>   On that great grief, that crown of thorn:
> See there, in deep amaze,
>   Thy sentence borne.
> To Thee, O Saviour Lord,
>   Who washed in blood our sins away,
> Our boundless gratitude
>   Its thanks would pay.

Day 72

Monday

Life more abundant

"I have come that they may have life, and that they may have it more abundantly." (John 10:10)

I read once about a beautiful eagle that was kept in a large cage in a zoo. People admired the imprisoned bird that was meant to soar into the heavens. One day the cage door was left open and the great bird walked out into freedom. But the years of imprisonment had robbed it of the power of flight, and it was soon returned to its tiny home.

It can be the painful experience of the Lord's people to cease to soar into the presence of God. We can confine ourselves to cages of our own making. I remember a dear and gifted brother who fell out with his brethren and never returned into fellowship with the Lord's people until he was in his mid-eighties. It was a joyous thing for him to come back. But many, many years of fellowship, contribution and service were lost, and he was called home not long after.

There are many things which can cause us distress or hurt, and which can prevent us from enjoying the salvation we have in Christ. But the Lord never wants us to lose the joy of our salvation, but to enjoy it to the full. Listen to His beautiful words, "I have come that they may have life, and that they may have it more abundantly."

Once we possess life in Christ, it cannot be taken from us: "And I give them eternal life, and they shall never perish; neither shall anyone snatch them out of My hand. My Father, who has given them to Me, is greater than all; and no one is able to snatch them out of My Father's hand" (John 10:28-29).

In the Tabernacle in the Old Testament, there was a table in the Holy Place. It was called the Table of Showbread. On it were kept twelve loaves of bread, representing the twelve tribes of Israel under the eye of God. What is interesting is that there was a crown of gold (Exodus 37:12, AV) which surrounded the loaves on the table, keeping them in place. What has always touched my heart is that the crown measured a hand's breadth – "neither shall anyone snatch them out of My hand … and no one is able to snatch them out of My Father's hand."

The Lord came so that we would have life and have it more abundantly. He described a full, rich, mature, fruitful and joyous life that had its source and security in the Son of God and God the Father and was sealed by the Spirit of God. As we wait to enter a new year, let us not be imprisoned by doubt or fear or circumstances. But let us see the days ahead, through the open door of God's grace, as a runway from which, set free by faith, we soar every day into the presence of God and are empowered to live to the full the lives He has given us. Unlike the eagle, we never lose the ability to fly, only the faith to do so: "Do not be afraid; only believe" (Luke 8:50).

Day 73

Tuesday

Knowing Christ's power

"Do not be afraid; only believe." (Luke 8:50)

Peter, James and John were chosen by the Lord to be with Him on three memorable occasions. They witnessed the power of Christ when He raised Jairus' daughter (Mark 5:35-43); the glory of Christ on the Mount of Transfiguration (Luke 9:28-36); and the sufferings of the love of Christ in the Garden of Gethsemane (Matthew 26:36-46). The Lord allowed Peter, James and John to see what others did not see. These experiences would sustain them in their circumstances, shape their ministry and be used to encourage the flock of God. These themes marked the brief testimony of James, the long life of His brother, John, and the bold witness of their friend, Peter. They are themes we need to be reminded of as we enter into new circumstances. We are about to embark on a journey through another day of our lives. We do not know what lies ahead of us, but we know the Saviour, and we can say with Paul, "I know whom I have believed and am persuaded that He is able to keep what I have committed to Him until that Day" (2 Timothy 1:12).

The raising of Jairus' daughter teaches us about Christ's power. The way the Lord reveals His power is very instructive. It starts with Jairus coming to Jesus. He went to the Lord at a time of crisis. Crises should never drive us away from God but towards Him. But coming into the Lord's presence is not restricted to wanting Him to address our needs. Coming to the Saviour fulfils the reason we exist. We were made for fellowship with God. Adam had everything provided for Him in Eden, and God came into the garden to have fellowship with the first man.

Through Christ, we have been brought into nearness with God, not only to know His mercy and provision but to know Him.

The Lord did not need to be in Jairus' house to heal his daughter, but he took Jairus on a journey of faith. What he experienced walking with the Lord to his home would stay with him for the rest of His life. I am sure that at the time Jairus wished that journey would have been as short as possible. But instead, it was slowed down by the need of another person, a diseased woman whose life was also in crisis. The Lord has time for every need, and just because our needs sometimes take longer to be dealt with than we would like, it does not mean the Saviour does not care. The delay brought the news of the death of Jairus' daughter. Things did not get better, but worse, and the rest of the journey seemed pointless in the eyes of many. But it provided the opportunity for the Lord to say to Jairus, "Do not be afraid; only believe."

It takes a long time for us to learn the pace at which the Lord moves. I remember being in the hospital for ultrasound treatment on a kidney stone. The doctor explained to me that the ultrasound waves were synchronised with the beat of my heart. God wants to synchronise the pace of our hearts with His. We do this by faith. The walk with Jairus continued until, at last, Jesus took the hand of his child. In John 11, Jesus spoke with a loud voice when He raised Lazarus to life. In the house of Jairus He spoke with gentle words, "Little girl, I say to you, arise." But the result was the same: life.

The world can often be frenzied and confusing and made all the worse when we pass through difficult circumstances. We become anxious and uncertain. The Lord wanted to teach His disciples Peter, James and John how to follow Him in faith and learn to walk with Him at His pace, assured of His gentle power and His peace reigning in their hearts. He wants to teach us the same lessons as we step into a new day.

Day 74

Wednesday

The mountaintop

Now it came to pass, about eight days after these sayings, that He took Peter, John, and James and went up on the mountain to pray. As He prayed, the appearance of His face was altered, and His robe became white and glistening. And behold, two men talked with Him, who were Moses and Elijah, who appeared in glory and spoke of His decease which He was about to accomplish at Jerusalem. (Luke 9:28-31)

I was at the funeral of a dear Indian brother who was one of the gentlest Christians I have known. At the service his nephew recalled a visit he had made to the UK to stay with his uncle. The uncle took him to see the Lake District and together they climbed one of the hills. It was a steep climb, the young man found the going tough and he was not enjoying the experience. When his uncle saw he was tired, he stopped and asked his nephew to turn round and look at the view. He remembered how his breath was taken away as he looked down on the beauties of the Lakes. As they continued and arrived at another vantage point, they would stop to take in what they could not see when they were in the valley below. He related the story as an illustration of the spiritual help his uncle was to him during his life.

The Lord always wants to take us higher. He does not want us to be earthbound, but to be taken up to where He is and empowered to live for Him in this world. Moses' face shone because of his mountaintop experience with God. And Jesus Christ took Peter, James and John to the top of another mountain, not to look down, but to see the glory of Christ and hear the Father's pleasure in His Son and His command to listen to Him.

How does this relate to our daily living? The overwhelming evidence from the people of God in the Old Testament is that their spiritual power came from the revelation of God to their hearts through His word. In the New Testament we read in John 1, "And the Word became flesh and dwelt among us, and we beheld His glory, the glory as of the only begotten of the Father, full of grace and truth" (v. 14). God came down. The moral glory of the Lord Jesus Christ as a man was seen in this world. His power witnessed to His deity. The transfiguration was about being taken up into a place where the disciples saw His intrinsic glory. Moses and Elijah were on the mountain with Him, not as equal with the Lord, but representing the Law and the Prophets that bore testimony to His sufferings, which they talked of, and His glory. They disappear, and the Father declares His pleasure in His Son. Peter would write about this at the end of his life, "For we did not follow cunningly devised fables when we made known to you the power and coming of our Lord Jesus Christ, but were eyewitnesses of His majesty. For He received from God the Father honour and glory when such a voice came to Him from the Excellent Glory: 'This is My beloved Son, in whom I am well pleased'. And we heard this voice which came from heaven when we were with Him on the holy mountain" (2 Peter 1:16-18).

A day is coming when we shall behold the glory of the Lord and be changed into His likeness (1 John 3). Now we have the privilege of communion with Christ through the abiding Spirit of God and reading and listening to the word of God. What we learn we take into our daily lives. This was the experience that moved the apostles, the early Christians and Christians throughout the generations. We don't need to climb a mountain but just find the time to enter His presence in worship, listen to His word and follow our Saviour.

Day 75

Thursday

Fellowship and fruitfulness

They said to Him, "Rabbi" (which is to say, when translated, Teacher), "where are You staying?" He said to them, "Come and see." (John 1:38-39)

"Abide with us, for it is toward evening, and the day is far spent." And He went in to stay with them. (Luke 24:29)

It is interesting to compare the Lord's first disciples' experience at the beginning of John's Gospel with that of the two on the road to Emmaus in Luke 24, after the Lord's resurrection. It seems the Holy Spirit is reinforcing the connection between fellowship with the Lord and the fruitfulness which emerges from it.

In John 1, Andrew and his friend follow Jesus. Following the Lord leads to fellowship with the Lord. We can follow at a distance, and hesitantly. But once we take those steps of faith, seeking to know the Saviour, He quickly draws us closer. Jesus had asked them what they wanted, and they replied, "Where are you staying?" This simple conversation begins a relationship with the Lord which would last the rest of their lives, and take them into eternity. The Lord's invitation to "come and see" is a vital one. It is by coming into the Lord's presence that our spiritual eyes are opened. This principle is fundamental to the Christian pathway. To deepen our knowledge of Christ, we must come and see; to become more faithful disciples, we must come and see; to know the will of God, we must come and see. Our minds and understanding are opened by the Holy Spirit's application of God's word to our hearts. The result is fruitfulness. In the case of Andrew, it immediately led him to bring Peter to Christ. This is an aspect of fruitfulness we should not overlook. Knowing the Saviour produces within us a desire to bring others to Christ. As a young Christian, I was impressed by a series of books by G.F. Dempster, including "Finding Men for Christ". They record the author's commitment to a ministry of personal evangelism and were a great encouragement to being guided by Christ, as one's faith is shared.

In Luke 24, as the Lord "made as though He would have gone further" (AV), the two disciples invited Him into their home. (It is a very well-known passage of Scripture. But familiarity with Scripture should never rob us of the depth of learning we find in the most uncomplicated narrative, nor should we despise its repeated teaching.) It is critical to our spiritual blessing that the Lord should be the centre of our hearts and homes. It is the experience of the Lord in our personal lives that produces fruitfulness in our fellowship. The Lord's revelation of the Scriptures to His disciples' hearts led to a desire in them not to lose His company. In their home, they saw the risen Saviour. This immediately led to them to share their experience with their fellow disciples. Their fruitfulness was ministering the living Christ to their brothers and sisters in Christ. It resulted in Him being at the centre of the hearts of His people (v. 36).

John 1 and Luke 24 teach us the Lord is central to our hearts, home, witness and fellowship. Each day we need to hear His words, "Come and see" and be encouraged to share our faith in Him, and to have hearts which appeal to the Lord to "abide with us" in every aspect of our lives.

Day 76

Friday

Manna from heaven

I am the living bread which came down from heaven.

(John 6:51)

Last Lord's Day, I was encouraged by the ministry of one of my oldest friends on the subject of manna. I have always found that the thoughts of fellow Christians give food for further reflection. The first place to which God took His people as they began their wilderness journey was the waters of Marah. He taught them at the very beginning of the 40 years which lay ahead of them that, whatever they faced, He would bring blessing out of bitterness and reveal Himself as "the Lord, your healer" (Exodus 15:26, ESV). It is a word for us today.

Then He leads them to the beautiful oasis that was Elim to demonstrate His love for them. From this place of refreshment and plenty, they go into the wilderness of Sin between Elim and Sinai. Here we get an insight into how quickly the people forgot the cruelty and violence of their slavery in Egypt. Their whole experience of God was one which demonstrated His care, power and blessing, but once things became arduous, the people complained bitterly. They thought, because their circumstances had changed, God had changed. It is a vital lesson for us to learn that circumstances do change dramatically, as we are learning, but we are to express our faith in our God who does not change. God responded to the complaints of the children of Israel by promising to rain bread from heaven. And He began supplying fresh manna every morning. That supply lasted for the next forty years, until they reached the borders of the Promised Land.

We used to go to a small Christian house party in the South of France in the late summer. Every morning the local baker would come in his old Citroën van with freshly baked bread. We would go to his vehicle to buy our daily provisions. This always reminded me of the manna sent from heaven! But it was different. We did not pick the bread off the ground: we took it from the hand of the person who made it. It is so important to see that God provided the manna, but the people had to collect it for themselves at the beginning of the day. Moses reminds the children of Israel that "God ... humbled you, allowed you to hunger, and fed you with manna which you did not know nor did your fathers know, that He might make you know that man shall not live by bread alone; but man lives by every word that proceeds from the mouth of the LORD" (Deuteronomy 8:2-3). He taught them the manna was not only a provision of food, but a daily reminder to live their lives by the word of God.

This has an exact bearing on our own pathway of faith. God provides in His word the spiritual food we need each day and delivers it personally to each of our hearts through the Holy Spirit. But we have to be there to receive it. He doesn't give it to us hastily, or to make us more knowledgeable about the Scriptures. He feeds our souls on the Person of Christ who said, "I am the bread of life ... I am the living bread which came down from heaven. If anyone eats of this bread, he will live forever" (see John 6:48-58). We are invited at the beginning of each new day to come into the presence of God and to open His word so that the Holy Spirit can reveal Jesus Christ to our hearts, and we can hear the voice of the Father saying, "This is My beloved Son. Hear him" (Luke 9:35). In this atmosphere, we worship, deepen our knowledge of the Saviour, understand the mind and will of God, pray intelligently and expectantly, and we are prepared for the day ahead.

Day 77

Saturday

Come aside

And He said to them, "Come aside by yourselves to a deserted place and rest a while." (Mark 6:31)

At the beginning of Mark 6 the Lord sent out His twelve disciples two by two on a preaching and healing mission. Later in the chapter (v. 30), they return and tell the Lord what they have done. It is then the Lord says to them, "Come aside by yourselves to a deserted place and rest a while." In this verse, the Lord describes His concern that we build into our lives times of reflection and rest, through which we are re-energised to continue to serve Him more effectively.

The Lord sent His disciples out in twos. In the service of God, fellowship is vital. We should complement each other as we serve and use our abilities and gifts in harmony. Natural abilities include, amongst other things, leadership qualities, strength, problem solving, and friendliness. These abilities need to be sanctified and brought under the Lordship of Christ. In this way, natural skills can be used spiritually. We also have spiritual gifts which are given to us to fulfil our place in the body of Christ. Both need to be used selflessly to glorify God in reaching out with the Gospel and building up the people of God. The other benefit of serving together is that we share the workload. This requires grace and humility. Sometimes in the service of God, we can jealously guard what we consider to be our service and be unwilling to include others. On the other hand, we may feel overburdened and would love to have others help, but support is not forthcoming.

The Lord teaches us that it is necessary for spiritual service that we pause to consider the work we are involved in and reflect on what we have done and seek His guidance and blessing. Today the word "furlough" is in everyday use. It means "leave of absence". It is a word which I first heard as a young Christian to describe the times when missionaries returned to their own countries for a period. Universities have "sabbaticals", when every seven years a lecturer is given a year to pursue other studies, or write, or travel. The term comes from Leviticus 25, when God ensured the land had to rest. We still refer to "fallow land", where land is not farmed but rested and then reused. God Himself rested after His work of creation. Reflection and rest are not unproductive, but essential to healthy spiritual growth and fruitful service.

If we do not build in this principle of spiritual reflection and rest leading to rejuvenation, we suffer. Our service can become sterile, and we can find ourselves driven by duty, not love. If our days are filled with a frenzy of activity, we will burn out, the burden we carry will become too great for us, and we may experience a breakdown. There is a vital connection in Psalm 23 between verse 1 and verses 2 and 3. David did not lack anything, because the Lord taught Him to lie down and drink beside still waters. This was the basis of being re-energised, restored and of being led in paths of righteousness. He had to learn to be still to know how to be active. May we listen to the Lord's invitation and make time to "Come aside by yourselves to a deserted place and rest a while." And to discover, in a daily experience of the peace of His presence, our burdens lifted, vision refocussed, spirits refreshed and restored, so that we can better serve the Saviour in happy fellowship.

Day 78

Sunday

Rooted in love

*For He shall grow up before Him as a tender plant,
And as a root out of dry ground.* (Isaiah 53:2)

Pursue peace with all people, and holiness, without which no one will see the Lord: looking carefully lest anyone fall short of the grace of God; lest any root of bitterness springing up cause trouble, and by this many become defiled. (Hebrews 12:14-15)

During the COVID-19 pandemic I have been impressed by the deepening affection we have experienced amongst the people of God. The crisis has had widespread and traumatic effects around the world. But there is much evidence of tender-heartedness and a desire to support and encourage each other in challenging and testing times.

In Isaiah 53 the Saviour is described as a tender plant. He rises up in a sterile and spiritually bankrupt nation to dispense, not judgement, but grace: "And the Word became flesh and dwelt among us, and we beheld His glory, the glory as of the only begotten of the Father, full of grace and truth" (John 1:14). He displayed grace and truth in His humility, as the tender-hearted Son of Man. W.E. Vine points out that one of the words meaning "tender-hearted" literally means "of good-heartedness". Now, as His people, we are to be characterised by a love for each other that distinguishes us as the disciples of the Lord Jesus. Crisis draws us to the Saviour and, as a consequence, we are drawn nearer to each other. And the love that reigns in our hearts is spread abroad.

The Epistle to the Hebrews reminds us of the "dry ground" of difficult times. A picture is painted of inactivity and weakness. The hands are not engaged in work, and the knees are not able to support heavy loads. Have you ever watched those extraordinary athletes called weightlifters? Their backs and knees are always supported as they lift weights the human body was not designed to lift. Our knees are essential for lifting heavy weights. In Hebrews 12:12 they illustrate spiritual weakness. We are encouraged to "strengthen the hands which hang down, and the feeble knees". How do we do this? By lifting up holy hands (1 Timothy 2:8) in prayer and bowing down on our knees in prayer to become "strong in the Lord and in the power of His might" (Ephesians 6:10). In so doing, at the throne of grace, "we ... obtain mercy and find grace to help in time of need" (Hebrews 4:16). And we are enabled to walk the straight path of discipleship and pursue peace and holiness.

We are also warned to watch that we don't stop walking in the grace of God and allow bitterness to fill our hearts. On Wednesday 6 January 2021, in America, we had a shocking demonstration of what can happen when the bitterness of defeat overwhelms people. Bitterness can be caused by envy and self-seeking (James 3:14) and, whatever the cause, it can spread to damage our fellowship. Christ is to dwell in our hearts through faith and "being rooted and grounded in love" we can follow the instruction: "Let all bitterness, wrath, anger, clamour, and evil speaking be put away from you, with all malice. And be kind to one another, tender-hearted, forgiving one another, even as God in Christ forgave you" (Ephesians 3:17, 4:31-32).

Day 79

Monday

Leaving the love of God

Then Jesus, looking at him, loved him, and said to him, "One thing you lack: Go your way, sell whatever you have and give to the poor, and you will have treasure in heaven; and come, take up the cross, and follow Me." (Mark 10:21)

I was reading recently that Elon Musk had become the richest man in the world, with a fortune of over £136bn. It is difficult to understand such wealth. But it is measurable, and it will be left behind.

One day a rich man came running to Jesus, knelt before Him and asked a vital question, "Good Teacher, what shall I do that I may inherit eternal life?" It was a good start. He came to the Saviour with a great sense of urgency, a deep respect for the Lord and a serious question about eternal life. It was a rare and open display of genuine spiritual concern. In response, the Lord asks Him the most important question, "Why do you call Me good? No one is good but One, that is, God" and then He adds, "You know the commandments…"

The Lord's first question was not answered. But the man then said, "Teacher, all these things I have kept from my youth." I believe he said this, not out of pride or self-righteousness, but from a genuine and honest heart. The Lord reacted in a way which is rarely expressed so precisely in the Bible, "Then Jesus, looking at him, loved him." At that moment, this man looked into the face of Jesus Christ and experienced His love. But love is challenging, and there was one thing which held sway over this man's life – his wealth. Jesus appealed to him,

"Sell whatever you have and give to the poor, and you will have treasure in heaven; and come, take up the cross, and follow Me." The tragedy was that his great possessions were more important to him than the love of Christ.

The Lord exposed the condition of the man's heart by omitting the first and great commandment, "You shall love the Lord your God with all your heart, with all your soul, and with all your mind" (Matthew 22:37-38). He tested him by asking why He called Him good. The man calls the Lord "Good teacher" then, after the Lord pointed out to Him that only God is good, he just calls Jesus "Teacher". For all his qualities, the man did not understand the reason for the question, "Why do you call Me good? No one is good but One, that is, God." Jesus wanted him to understand that the lowly Nazarene who never owned a home or carried a penny was God. His riches could never be calculated, and were eternal. He created and sustained everything. Jesus looked on this man and loved him. That was the moment for him to discover he could never love the Lord his God with all his heart, with all his soul, and with all his mind. He needed a Saviour. But it was also the moment to discover that the Son of God loved him and wanted him to receive eternal life. But his wealth would not allow him to be blessed. He was very sorrowful and walked away from the love of Christ.

Thank God that, through His immense grace, we have come to know who Christ truly is, and His love for us. He removed all the distance that separated us from His love. He enabled us to respond in faith to that love that will not let us go and that sustains us as we seek to take up His cross and follow Him. We could not be richer.

Day 80

Tuesday

Coming to the Saviour

And throwing aside his garment, he rose and came to Jesus.

(Mark 10:50)

There is a remarkable contrast between the circumstances surrounding the rich man who came to Jesus and what happened on Jericho's outskirts at the end of the chapter. The differences between the rich man and blind Bartimaeus were profound. The rich man ran to Jesus, knelt down before Him and had His complete attention. Bartimaeus could not run to the Saviour and kneel in worship. He was not even a face in the vast crowd that surrounded Jesus and His disciples. He could not stand and watch but had to sit where he was. No one was concerned with his plight.

But Bartimaeus was not deaf. He clearly heard that Jesus was passing by. It seems the rich man saw the Lord near Jerusalem, a city of blessing. Blind Bartimaeus begged outside Jericho, the city whose future rebuilder was cursed by Joshua at the end of Joshua 6. The rich man had great possessions; Bartimaeus had nothing. There were no obstacles to the rich man reaching Jesus. But Bartimaeus had to overcome those who would try to stop his cry of faith. He was the son of Timaeus, a name derived from the Greek word *timao* meaning "to honour".

When he heard Jesus of Nazareth was passing by, he cried out to the Saviour. The rich man had called Jesus "Good teacher" and later only "teacher". Bartimaeus knew it was Jesus of Nazareth who was passing by. He was passing by because He was Jesus of Nazareth. From that lowly town (ESV), He emerged as the

Saviour of the world. It was a title He was never ashamed of because it spoke of His coming down into the poverty and need of this world. Bartimaeus cried out, "Jesus, Son of David, have mercy on me!" The Lord is spoken of as the Servant of God in Mark's Gospel. There is no genealogy given. A servant's genealogy was rarely referred to even if it was known. But Bartimaeus identifies Jesus as the Son of David, great David's greater son. In Matthew 22:41-46, Jesus confounded the Pharisees by asking them whose son the Christ was. They said, "The Son of David." The Lord quoted Psalm 110:1:

> The LORD said to my Lord,
> "Sit at My right hand,
> Till I make Your enemies Your footstool."

But the Lord points out, "If then David calls him Lord, how is he his son?" (ESV).

Jesus is the Son of God, the King of kings and the Son of Man. The Pharisees knew that Christ was the Son of David by lineage, but did not understand His deity or believe Jesus was the Christ. Bartimaeus' heart was full of faith and he could not be silenced as he called out to Jesus Christ, the Son of David, for mercy.

In his need, the voice of the blind, poor and helpless beggar gave honour to Jesus as the Christ, the Son of David. In response, Jesus stood still and commanded him to be called. The rich man could not give up his great possessions to come to Jesus. Bartimaeus gave up what seemed to be his only possession to go to Jesus: "throwing aside his garment, he rose and came to Jesus" and received his sight. The Lord honoured his faith. He had not seen the face of Jesus looking in love upon him as the rich ruler had. But as his eyes were immediately opened, he saw Jesus. His life was transformed, and he joyfully followed his Saviour. This morning may our hearts be lifted in worship to honour the Saviour and remember the depth of His love which brought Him to where we were so we would come to Him.

Day 81

Wednesday

Fruit in old age

They shall still bear fruit in old age;
They shall be fresh and flourishing. *(Psalm 92:14)*

I became a grandparent over 20 years ago, and it is comforting to know that Paul encourages us to care for the aged. In 1 Timothy 5:4 he writes, "But if any widow has children or grandchildren, let them first learn to show piety at home and to repay their parents; for this is good and acceptable before God." It was part of the Church's testimony to care particularly for the aged and vulnerable amongst them. We read in Psalm 68:5:

A father of the fatherless, a defender of widows,
Is God in His holy habitation.

God reminds His people to ensure young and old were cared for when they were destitute. It is interesting to note that great servants like Stephen and Philip were involved in this care. From the words spoken at the cross we learn that Joseph had died, and the Lord, as the eldest son in His family, places His mother, Mary, into John's care.

Age teaches us about dependency, growing weakness and frailty. Old age seems so distant until we suddenly find ourselves unable to do all the things we took for granted. During times of insecurity, we need our family, and brothers and sisters in Christ, not just to do something for us, but to be valued and included. But the Bible also explains the things we can do. We read in Deuteronomy 4:9: "Only take heed to yourself, and diligently keep yourself, lest you forget the things your eyes have seen, and lest they depart from your heart all the days of your life. And teach them to your children and your grandchildren." I was privileged to grow up in the same home as my grandparents and my great-grandmother. I have never forgotten seeing first-hand the hard work, commitment, sacrifice and love that went in caring for the elderly. But I also witnessed the wisdom of old age.

I was once talking to a very able Christian with broad business experience. He gave the impression that his father, who was not highly educated or widely travelled, had little to teach him. I questioned this, pointing out that his father, a very godly man, had a life of enormous value and much to teach his children about spiritual matters that could well influence his business life. It is easy to dismiss aged people as having nothing to contribute to today's fast-moving world when they have much to impart, if we had the time to stop, listen and learn.

It is interesting that in old age you can feel that your time is running out. On the other hand, we move into an area of life where we have greater control of our time. We can invest our time and resources into praying for, encouraging and being examples to succeeding generations. Timothy gained a great deal from his grandmother: "I call to remembrance the genuine faith that is in you, which dwelt first in your grandmother Lois and your mother Eunice, and I am persuaded is in you also" (2 Timothy 1:5). This beautiful verse demonstrates the harmony of two generations in the spiritual upbringing of a child. These women were so influential in Timothy becoming a great servant of God. I read some months ago of a Christian known to friends who started a ministry amongst refugees in Greece. He was in his nineties! This dear brother, and Lois the grandmother of Timothy, are such encouragements for us to value the aged saints of God and for them to "bear fruit in old age" and remarkably to be "fresh and flourishing" (Psalm 92:14).

Day 82

Thursday

I hope in Him

*Through the LORD's mercies, we are not consumed,
Because His compassions fail not.
They are new every morning;
Great is Your faithfulness.
"The LORD is my portion," says my soul,
"Therefore I hope in Him!"* (Lamentations 3:22-24)

The Book of Lamentations was written by Jeremiah, the "weeping prophet". He laments the destruction of Jerusalem by Babylon in 586 BC and the desolation of Judah. It has struck me that in the most painful experiences recorded in the Bible you find the most beautiful expressions of hope amid despair. In just thirty words the prophet, by the Holy Spirit, speaks of God's mercy, compassion, faithfulness, presence and hope. He did this when faith was under enormous pressure, and people were asking "Where is God?"

As we went through the bitter experience of COVID-19, simultaneously people passed through all the other experiences of life that cause distress but had nothing to do with the pandemic. It is at these times people lose faith and hope and feel abandoned. It was in such circumstances the prophet wrote the short verses we have read this morning. These words have touched the hearts of millions of people for nearly 2500 years.

Mercy is about meeting needs. Our needs are not only material, but also spiritual. Jeremiah discovered God's mercy was still active in the midst of destruction and prevented His nation from being obliterated. Throughout the Lord Jesus' ministry,

He found people in hopeless situations, and in mercy met their needs. He removed the power of disaster, the devil, disease and death. It is one thing to have the power to remove needs, it is another to express compassion – which is about feeling another's pain in my heart. Those who Jesus found, and those who came to Him, did not only experience mercy, but also knew they were loved. Sometimes, as we have discovered, individuals walked away from the Saviour because their faith in a material world was greater than their willingness to know the love of God.

But God's compassion does not fail, and His faithfulness is new every morning. When I started writing these daily posts, I woke up to the light of a new day and the singing of my blackbird friend. Now I wake up to darkness, and I don't hear a song. But I still thank God for His faithfulness. I am assured of the faithfulness of His mercy that we find at the Throne of Grace and the faithfulness of His compassionate heart as we pass through challenging times.

I recently wrote to a young friend that I expected to struggle through lockdown. Our active lives came to an abrupt halt and the celebrations of what should have been a special year were taken from us. And so many others have passed through far more bitter experiences. But during the restrictions of COVID-19 I discovered what Jeremiah wrote: "The Lord is my portion." Our lives are distilled down to what is most precious and where our hope lies: "Therefore I hope in Him!" The faith which emerged from the ruins of Jerusalem set in motion events which are still taking place, and leading to the time when

> the earth will be filled
> With the knowledge of the glory of the Lord,
> As the waters cover the sea (Habakkuk 2:14).

Hope in Him!

Day 83

Friday

God's faithfulness, living faith and focussed prayer

But constant prayer was offered to God for him by the church.

(Acts 12:5)

It is interesting that whilst the church in Jerusalem constantly prayed for Peter, he was fast asleep. What seemed to be his last evening on earth was not going to interrupt a good night's rest! Even the angel had to make an effort to wake him up.

The circumstances surrounding Peter's imprisonment and his deliverance from king Herod teach us a lot about God's faithfulness, living faith and focussed prayer.

First, we have God's faithfulness. The Lord had a purpose for Peter's life. He had told him at the end of John's Gospel, "Most assuredly, I say to you, when you were younger, you girded yourself and walked where you wished; but when you are old, you will stretch out your hands, and another will gird you and carry you where you do not wish" (John 21:18). No matter how powerful the monarch or tyrant, they cannot overrule the will of God. Peter was going to die a martyr. But it was not Herod who decided when that would happen; it was God. Our times are in His hands.

Peter had a living faith in Christ. He had not always listened carefully to what the Lord said. More than once, Peter thought he knew better. Even when God was calling him to bring the Gospel to the Gentiles, he said, "Not so Lord" (Acts 10:14). But that was not the case in Herod's jail. There he proved his living faith by falling asleep. Like David, he was saying,

> I will both lie down in peace, and sleep;
> For You alone, O Lord, make me dwell in safety
> (Psalm 4:8).

Living faith is not always expressed by activity, but by trusting God throughout our lives with all its testing circumstances.

The church was focussed on praying for Peter, continually asking for him to be delivered from Herod. Last night I was at our local prayer meeting – on Zoom, of course – and we prayed for many different people who were on our hearts. It is incredible how the mention of someone's name brings them vividly before our minds. And I thought of how, when we approach the Throne of Grace with people's names on our lips, the whole of their beings are embraced in the mind and care of God. *We* remember much; *He* knows everything. And God will fulfil His perfect will in each of our lives. We should be clearly focussed on what we will pray about in our private prayers and in our prayer meetings. And we should not overlook the importance of single-issue prayer meetings.

What was extraordinary about this event in Peter's life was that faith was expressed in prison, but faith did not fill the prayer meeting! But thank God for Rhoda, who was filled with gladness for answered prayer when she saw Peter, but doubted by her fellow Christians (Acts 12:14). God indicates Peter's trust in the Lord as he slept soundly. He also tells us about the importance of constantly praying for the things He lays on our hearts and assures us He will answer our prayers, even when we doubt. Finally, He teaches us to have a confidence in Him that believes He will listen and respond to our prayers. As we approach the wonderful Throne of Grace, may we come boldly, pray clearly, appeal constantly, trust completely, rest peacefully, praise thankfully and worship gladly the One who says, "Ask in My name" (John 14:13).

Day 84

Saturday

Building, praying, keeping and looking

But you, beloved, building yourselves up on your most holy faith, praying in the Holy Spirit, keep yourselves in the love of God, looking for the mercy of our Lord Jesus Christ unto eternal life.

(Jude 20-21)

Jude gives us a lot to think about in these two verses. First, he affectionately encourages us to build ourselves up on our most holy faith. I have a series of exercises I do each morning to ensure that I don't lose mobility in my advancing years. If I miss a few days, the workouts seem that much harder. Building up needs commitment. Jude describes our faith as "most holy". It is founded in Christ, and brought us into all the blessings we have in Him. We must never take it for granted, but be committed to growing in it. In his final address to the Ephesian elders, Paul commends them to "God and to the word of His grace, which is able to build you up" (Acts 20:32). Jude, however, emphasises our responsibility for our own spiritual well-being.

Secondly, Jude encourages us to pray in the Holy Spirit. We must not overcomplicate these words. The Holy Spirit's ministry is to glorify Christ in our hearts and lives. Praying in the Holy Spirit is to be led to pray for those things that glorify Christ in our hearts and empower us to faithfully follow and serve Him. The Spirit of God will always take us in the right direction (Acts 16:6-10). Our prayers should be guided by the One who "makes intercession for the saints according to the will of God" (Romans 8:26-27). In this way we discover the mind of Christ and the blessing of God.

Thirdly, we are to keep ourselves in the love of God. This means that we are always to be conscious of God's love resting upon us and persuaded that we cannot be separated from "the love of God, which is in Christ Jesus our Lord" (Romans 8:39). This assurance is given by the word of God and the Spirit of God. God's Spirit pours the love of God into our hearts (Romans 5:5). When our grandchildren were young, we often took them to the seaside. They never tired of going to the sea to fill their buckets. The sea was vast, and no matter how many times they filled their tiny buckets, it never got smaller. But the delight and pleasure they got from their buckets full of seawater ensured they went back to the source again and again. So it is with us. As we enjoy and draw on God's love, it fills our hearts and overflows in witness to the God of all grace.

Finally, we look for "the mercy of our Lord Jesus Christ unto eternal life". The blessings of faith in Christ are not confined to the present, but embrace the future. Our "citizenship is in heaven, from which we also eagerly wait for the Saviour, the Lord Jesus Christ" (Philippians 3:20). God, in Christ, reached down to us in all the richness of His mercy (Ephesians 2:4). That work of salvation will be fully accomplished when by that same rich mercy Christ will take His own out of the world to bring them into the Father's house, and our home, in heaven (John 14:1-3). Jude encourages us to live in anticipation of that day and never cease to build ourselves up in Christ, pray in fellowship with the Holy Spirit, and keep ourselves in the love of God.

Day 85

Sunday

The Name of Jesus

Therefore God also has highly exalted Him and given Him the name which is above every name, that at the name of Jesus every knee should bow, of those in heaven, and of those on earth, and of those under the earth, and that every tongue should confess that Jesus Christ is Lord, to the glory of God the Father.

(Philippians 2:9-11)

It was a wonderful day when, from the presence of God, Gabriel appeared in despised Nazareth to announce to Mary she would have a Son called Jesus. Joseph learned in a dream about Mary's Son and was given the responsibility for calling the child Jesus, "for He will save His people from their sins" (Matthew 1:21).

The full name of King Charles III is Charles Philip Arthur George. The name of the Son of God, the creator of all things, is simply Jesus. To the people of God this despised name immediately raises in our hearts the wonder of divine love. He also has the title "Jesus of Nazareth", which simultaneously describes His profound power over His creation, His lowly grace, and His ministry of love, healing, forgiveness and salvation.

This morning, it is Jesus who gathers us together: "For where two or three are gathered together in My name, I am there in the midst of them" (Matthew 18:20). His name was not invented on earth. It was given from heaven, and the mention of it fills our hearts with the wonder of a journey from glory into the world He made, to reveal the heart of God. We follow Jesus afresh in recalling His birth, childhood, and ministry of grace and truth. We read the title above the cross, "This is Jesus of

Nazareth, the King of the Jews." We remember Joseph "went to Pilate and asked for the body of Jesus. Then he took it down, wrapped it in linen, and laid it in a tomb that was hewn out of the rock, where no one had ever lain before" (Luke 23:52-53). We rejoice to read of Jesus' resurrection: "Jesus Himself stood in the midst of them, and said to them, 'Peace to you'" (Luke 24:36) and we bow down and join Thomas in worshipping Jesus as our Lord and God.

On the mount of Olives, we hear the angels speaking again of another day when Jesus would come down, "This same Jesus, who was taken up from you into heaven, will so come in like manner as you saw Him go into heaven." And by faith we understand that God has highly exalted His Son and given Him a name above every name. And there is a coming day when, at the name of Jesus, every knee shall bow, of those in heaven, and of those on earth, and of those under the earth, and that every tongue shall confess that Jesus Christ is Lord, to the glory of God the Father (Philippians 2:10-11). In the meantime, we live our lives "looking unto Jesus" (Hebrews 12:2). Like the once blind Bartimaeus, we follow Jesus (Mark 10:52).

Jesus said, "Ask in my name" (John 14:13; also 15:16, 16:23-24,26). We have the privilege of approaching the Father in all the majesty and power of the name of Jesus. His name is "like perfume poured out" (Song of Solomon 1:3, NIV), and today we have a fresh opportunity to bow in worship before our Saviour and our Lord, full of gratitude and praise:

> LORD Jesus, gladly do our lips express
> Our hearts' deep sense of all Thy worthiness
> (T. Willey).

Day 86

Monday

The poor in spirit

*"Blessed are the poor in spirit,
For theirs is the kingdom of heaven."* (Matthew 5:3)

These are the first words Jesus spoke to His disciples as He sat down on the mountainside in Matthew 5. What follows has become known as the Sermon on the Mount. I want to reflect on the words of the Lord on that occasion. Each verse begins with the word "Blessed". It means 'happy, because in receipt of God's favour', and the Lord uses it to describe the character of those blessed and the nature of their blessing.

When the Lord speaks about the poor in spirit, He does not speak of those who are materially poor. The most helpful insight into His meaning is what we find in Isaiah 57:15:

> For thus says the High and Lofty One
> Who inhabits eternity, whose name is Holy:
> "I dwell in the high and holy place,
> With him who has a contrite and humble spirit,
> To revive the spirit of the humble,
> And to revive the heart of the contrite ones."

The poor in spirit are those who recognise their need and look outside of themselves for salvation. This is the experience we have when we come to the Saviour – an overwhelming sense of our spiritual poverty and need of Him. Peter had this experience in Luke 5:1-11. In this chapter, the Lord had taught a large crowd of people from the disciple's boat. Afterwards He told them to launch into the deep and fish. Peter explained to the Lord that they had fished all night and caught nothing. He knew the Lake of Gennesaret well and felt he was wasting his time launching out again. Peter did not understand that the Person who spoke to him was the One who made the lake and everything in it. Peter did what the Lord asked out of politeness, but thinking he knew better. The fishermen were overwhelmed by the catch of fish they had as a result of obeying the Lord. But the most profound impression was in Peter's heart. He knew he was not worthy to be in the presence of the Lord. He felt poor in spirit and humbled as he discovered his own heart. It was not the last time this would happen. He was in the presence of the One who inhabits eternity and whose name is Holy. Peter felt his unholiness. The Lord's greatness brought Peter into the place of contrition and humility and to the entrance to blessing.

Isaiah also wrote,

> "To revive the spirit of the humble,
> And to revive the heart of the contrite ones."

The Lord's next words were, "Do not be afraid. From now on you will catch men" (v. 10). The Saviour takes a headstrong fisherman and begins to transform him into the lowly shepherd who encourages us powerfully and beautifully: "Humble yourselves under the mighty hand of God, that He may exalt you in due time, casting all your care upon Him, for He cares for you" (1 Peter 5:6-7). The great lesson Peter teaches us is that the humility we learned at the cross should always characterise us as the children of God. Our strength and power are found in the Saviour. Now, like those fishermen so long ago, it is our business to forsake all and follow the Saviour and prove the blessedness of the life we have in Him.

Day 87

Tuesday

The mourners

*"Blessed are those who mourn,
For they shall be comforted."* (Matthew 5:4)

The Lord Jesus uses the word "mourn" to describe those who feel the effects and consequences of living in a suffering world. We mourn when we lose someone we love. And we also mourn over other painful experiences, regrets and mistakes. It is not something we feel only in our own circumstances, but also in those of others. It is possible to travel through the world desensitised to its suffering and distress. But such an attitude should not characterise Christians. The Lord never walked through the world in this way. He was "a Man of sorrows and acquainted with grief" (Isaiah 53:3), because He felt our needs in His heart. Mourning is a genuine experience, and it causes us to pause, reflect and learn. In Psalm 69:20 we read of Christ:

> Reproach has broken my heart,
> And I am full of heaviness;
> I looked for someone to take pity, but there was none;
> And for comforters, but I found none.

Yet we discover that God is the source of comfort. The Holy Spirit is called the Comforter (John 14:16, AV). In Acts 9:31 we read: "The churches throughout all Judea, Galilee, and Samaria had peace and were edified. And walking in the fear of the Lord and in the comfort of the Holy Spirit, they were multiplied." The Epistle to the Romans teaches us about the comfort of the Scriptures: "For whatever things were written before were written for our learning, that we through the patience and comfort of the Scriptures might have hope" (Romans 15:4).

We are also comforted through the ministry of God's word (1 Corinthians 14:3).

God is the God of all comfort, and through Jesus Christ and the Holy Spirit He ministers to us in circumstances which cause us to mourn. In addressing our distress, He not only comforts us and strengthens us to carry on, but also wants us to become comforters: "Blessed be the God and Father of our Lord Jesus Christ, the Father of mercies and God of all comfort, who comforts us in all our tribulation, that we may be able to comfort those who are in any trouble, with the comfort with which we ourselves are comforted by God" (2 Corinthians 1:3-4).

Mourning is not a fruitless experience. Through it we face the sorrows and pain of life, and, as 2 Corinthians 1 explains, it has a refining effect upon us. By knowing the presence and power of the God of comfort, we can be transformed into those who can comfort and support others in their sufferings.

The Lord Jesus describes His ministry in Luke 4:18-19 by quoting Isaiah 61:1-2a. This passage goes on to say:

> "To console those who mourn in Zion,
> To give them beauty for ashes,
> The oil of joy for mourning,
> The garment of praise for the spirit of heaviness" (v. 3).

Mourning is not a destination; it is a part of a journey that leads to the day when "God shall wipe away all tears from their eyes; and there shall be no more death, neither sorrow, nor crying, neither shall there be any more pain: for the former things are passed away" (Revelation 21:4, AV).

Day 88

Wednesday

The meek

*"Blessed are the meek,
For they shall inherit the earth."* *(Matthew 5:5)*

Jesus Christ was characterised by lowliness. He was, as we saw yesterday, "a Man of sorrows", and He says of Himself "I am gentle (meek)" Matthew 11:29. In Matthew 21, when the Lord Jesus entered Jerusalem as its rightful King, it was in fulfilment of the prophecy in Zechariah 9:9:

> Rejoice greatly, O daughter of Zion; shout, O daughter of Jerusalem: behold, thy King cometh unto thee: he is just, and having salvation; lowly (meek), and riding upon an ass, and upon a colt the foal of an ass (AV).

His righteousness and power to save were demonstrated in meekness.

Meekness is an outward expression of inward power. It is the joyful acceptance of the mind and will of God for our lives and demonstrates an implicit trust in His blessing in all circumstances. Meekness is living in the reality and power of Romans 8:28: "And we know that all things work together for good to those who love God, to those who are the called according to His purpose."

We tend to mistake meekness for timidity. The original sense of "a gentleman" was a man of rank possessing a gentle, generous, and courageous character. Today the world often confuses loudness and self-assertion with power. Micah describes what God requires:

> To do justly,
> To love mercy,
> And to walk humbly with your God (Micah 6:8).

Proverbs 31:10-31 describes the characteristics of godly women and lists the attributes which emerge from walking in the fear of the Lord (v. 30). They are not the actions of timid people, but of fruitful and energetic lives.

Paul writes in Philippians 2:

> God also has highly exalted Him and given Him the name which is above every name, that at the name of Jesus every knee should bow, of those in heaven, and of those on earth, and of those under the earth, and that every tongue should confess that Jesus Christ is Lord, to the glory of God the Father (vv. 9-11).

The Lord expressed His kingship through meekness as He entered Jerusalem. In a future day the same Jesus will be owned as Lord of lords and King of kings. Today, from the glory of His majesty in heaven, He invites us to learn to become like Him in meekness and humility. He empowers us to live useful lives for Him. The Lord spoke to His disciples about the meek inheriting the earth. This will be seen perfectly in the Person of Christ in a coming day. And our inheritance is in Him.

> Walk worthy of the Lord, fully pleasing Him, being fruitful in every good work and increasing in the knowledge of God; strengthened with all might, according to His glorious power, for all patience and longsuffering with joy; giving thanks to the Father who has qualified us to be partakers of the inheritance of the saints in the light (Colossians 1:10-12).

By seeing Christ's majesty, the power of His meekness is revealed in us.

Day 89

Thursday

The hungry

"Blessed are those who hunger and thirst for righteousness, For they shall be filled." (Matthew 5:6)

The Father declared Jesus as His beloved Son, in whom He was well pleased (Matthew 3:17). Following the joy of that moment, and before entering His ministry of grace, Jesus goes into the wilderness. He is led there by the Holy Spirit and fasts (Matthew 4). In the Old Testament the people of God, at times of crisis, set everyday life aside and fasted and prayed to confess their failure and cast themselves upon God. The Lord Jesus goes into the wilderness in all the perfection of His Sonship. He demonstrates through His fasting His devotion to the Father and the fulfilling of His will, not living by bread alone, "but by every word that proceeds from the mouth of God" (v. 4). All the Beatitudes are seen perfectly in the Saviour. His hunger and thirst were to do the will of God. All our blessings come from His power to do this; "Behold, I have come to do Your will, O God" (Hebrews 10:9).

The Lord's ministry addressed unrighteousness. He constantly highlighted and judged the hypocrisy, legalism, and manifest failure of those responsible for the spiritual well-being of God's people. At the same time, He dedicated Himself to addressing, in grace and with humility, the needs which surrounded Him. At Sychar's well, wearied, hungry and thirsty, He leads one lost soul to Himself (John 4). Afterwards, His disciples encourage Him to eat. He replies, "I have food to eat of which you do not know", adding "My food is to do the will of Him who sent Me, and to finish His work" (John 4:34). On the Cross, the Lord

Jesus in all the exhaustion of His sufferings says, "I thirst." His next words were not words of exhaustion but of power: "It is finished" (John 19:28,30).

Before His resurrection, the Lord's disciples did not understand His total devotion to His Father's will. Nor in that devotion did they see the manifestation of the Father heart. Philip even asked Jesus to show them the Father. There is a sadness in the Lord's reply, "Have I been with you so long, and yet you have not known Me, Philip? He who has seen Me has seen the Father" (John 14:9). He is the brightness of His glory and the express image of His person (Hebrews 1:3).

In Christ, we discover "the kingdom of God is not eating and drinking, but righteousness and peace and joy in the Holy Spirit" (Romans 14:17), all attributes of the fruit of the Spirit of God. The Lord has made us righteous and set us free from sin to become "the slaves of righteousness" (Romans 6:19). We follow the Lord, in pursuing righteousness (1 Timothy 6:11 and 2 Timothy 2:22) and being guided in it by the word of God (2 Timothy 3:16). In 2 Timothy 4:8 we are promised a crown of righteousness.

This morning let us remember and worship our Saviour who is the "King of righteousness" and the "King of peace" (Hebrews 7:2), looking, with hope in our hearts, to the millennial day when righteousness will reign (Jeremiah 23:5) and on to the eternal day wherein righteousness will dwell (2 Peter 3:13).

And, in the meantime, may His love cause us to hunger and thirst for righteousness as we seek to be "filled with the fruits of righteousness which are by Jesus Christ, to the glory and praise of God" (Philippians 1:11).

Day 90

Friday

The merciful

*"Blessed are the merciful,
For they shall obtain mercy."* (Matthew 5:7)

Mercy is a practical response to another's need. The cost is borne by the person showing mercy. There also needs to be a willingness to receive the kindness being offered. True mercy seeks the welfare and good of others. The mercy of God has its source in His love: "But God, who is rich in mercy, because of His great love with which He loved us, even when we were dead in trespasses, made us alive together with Christ (by grace you have been saved)" (Ephesians 2:4-5).

This relationship with love is significant. A lawyer tested the Lord with the question, "Which is the great commandment in the law?" Jesus replied, "'You shall love the Lord your God with all your heart, with all your soul, and with all your mind.' This is the first and great commandment. And the second is like it: 'You shall love your neighbour as yourself.' On these two commandments hang all the Law and the Prophets" (Matthew 22:37-40). I think Jesus quoted the second commandment to challenge the heart of the questioner. Our behaviour towards others is a measure of our love for God. The lawyer was simply asking an academic question. The Lord was describing his life.

The Lord's ministry was characterised by mercy. It was shown to the broken-hearted, blind, deaf, mute, crippled, lame, diseased, frightened and hopeless, and it even conquered death. It was established in love and grace. But the time came, in the words of Psalm 69:20, when the Lord Jesus experienced reproach which broke His heart, and He could say,

> I am full of heaviness;
> I looked for someone to take pity, but there was none;
> And for comforters, but I found none.

The Person whose mercy ensured our salvation was never relieved in the sufferings it cost. Now, in resurrection glory, His ministry of mercy continues. He is our merciful and faithful High Priest (Hebrews 2:17), able to come to our aid in time of need with a heart which understands our sufferings and can relieve them:

> For we do not have a High Priest who cannot sympathise with our weaknesses, but was in all points tempted as we are, yet without sin. Let us therefore come boldly to the throne of grace, that we may obtain mercy and find grace to help in time of need (Hebrews 4:15-16).

Overwhelmingly in the New Testament, mercy is something which we receive from God in abundance. But in receiving such rich mercy, it compels us to show it. Today's verse establishes that we should be merciful. The Epistle to the Romans reminds us to show mercy with cheerfulness (Romans 12:8). James writes of the wisdom from above being full of mercy (James 3:17). In essence, we are encouraged to show mercy eagerly, cheerfully and plentifully.

In Luke 10, after telling the story of the Good Samaritan, the Lord asked the lawyer which person was neighbour to the man who fell among the thieves. The lawyer said, "He who showed mercy on him." Then Jesus said to him, "Go and do likewise." The Lord wasn't just challenging the lawyer: He was speaking to me.

Day 91

Saturday

The pure in heart

*"Blessed are the pure in heart,
For they shall see God."* (Matthew 5:8)

There can be a tendency to concentrate on the first part of today's verse in our desire to be pure in a world marked by spiritual and moral impurity. But we also need to consider the second part of the verse. The word "pure" here means cleansed. Only those redeemed by God and made holy through Christ's work see God. Now we see by faith. The Christian's hope in Christ will take us into the presence of God. We are introduced to both these thoughts at the beginning of John 14:

> "Let not your heart be troubled; you believe in God, believe also in Me. In My Father's house are many mansions; if it were not so, I would have told you. I go to prepare a place for you. And if I go and prepare a place for you, I will come again and receive you to Myself; that where I am, there you may be also" (vv. 1-3).

The phrase "pure in heart" also suggests "with undivided loyalty". The Lord makes Himself the object of our faith: "Believe also in Me." This is our present experience. We live by faith, as Paul describes in Galatians 2:20: "I have been crucified with Christ; it is no longer I who live, but Christ lives in me; and the life which I now live in the flesh I live by faith in the Son of God, who loved me and gave Himself for me."

In John 14 the Lord also promises to take His people into the Father's house. In John 17:24, Jesus prays to the Father that His

Church "may be with Me where I am, that they may behold My glory." Ephesians 5 explains that Christ loved the Church and gave Himself for her, and one day will present her to Himself as a glorious church. 1 Corinthians 15 and 1 Thessalonians 4 describe the day the redeemed company are brought into the Father's house. In that day, we shall enter into the completeness of our salvation and our eternal destiny.

When the Passover lamb was chosen, it was kept safe in order to demonstrate its perfection before its sacrifice (Exodus 12:6). Christ's purity, holiness and perfection were seen in His peerless life. And that life was given for us in love at Calvary. Now, in resurrection glory, He is the object of our faith. His love sustains us, and we witness to it in our lives.

In the opening verses of 1 John 3, the apostle beautifully describes God's love for us. He has made us His children and promised that we will be with Christ, and like Him, "for we shall see Him as He is". Then he adds, "And everyone who has this hope in Him (Christ) purifies himself, just as He is pure." The reality of Christ's return had a profound effect on the early Church. Christians lived in the reality of this hope. It shaped and enriched their lives. It purified them and enabled them to live, not in self-righteousness, but lives of sacrifice, purpose and witness. The pure in heart do not love the world, but they do live in the world. The word of God sanctifies us, and we are sent into the world by the Lord to be His witnesses (John 17:14-18). Christ's purifying ministry begins in our hearts, it purifies our lives and transforms us into His likeness. The world dismisses purity and suffers as a consequence. We rejoice in the One who is its source.

Day 92

Sunday

The peacemakers

"Blessed are the peacemakers,
For they shall be called sons of God."   *(Matthew 5:9)*

The Lord is the Great Peacemaker. Isaiah describes Immanuel in the following words:

> For unto us a Child is born,
> Unto us, a Son is given;
> And the government will be upon His shoulder.
> And His name will be called Wonderful, Counsellor, Mighty God,
> Everlasting Father, Prince of Peace (Isaiah 9:6).

After being healed of muteness, Zacharias, the father of John the Baptist, was filled with the Holy Spirit and prophesied of the coming Christ. He ended with the words:

> "Through the tender mercy of our God,
> With which the Dayspring from on high has visited us;
> To give light to those who sit in darkness and the shadow of death,
> To guide our feet into the way of peace"
> (Luke 1:78-79).

The Lord's birth was heralded by angels, saying,

> "Glory to God in the highest,
> And on earth peace, goodwill toward men!"
> (Luke 2:14).

The Lord dispensed peace wherever He went. In Mark chapters 4 and 5 we see this ministry so clearly. The wind is rebuked and He speaks to the sea, "Peace, be still!" – nature is at peace (Mark 4:39). Legion is set free from the power of Satan and is found sitting, clothed and in his right mind – a man is at peace (Mark 5:15). The diseased woman who could not be cured was healed, and the Lord said to her, "Daughter, your faith has made you well. Go in peace" – a woman was at peace (Mark 5:34). Jairus' daughter was raised from the dead: "Little girl, I say to you, arise" – a family was at peace (Mark 5:41). The Saviour intervenes in our circumstances and in our lives to bring peace.

Before going to the cross, the Lord Jesus gave His peace to His disciples (John 14:27). Upon the cross, He imparts peace to the heart of a dying thief: "Today you will be with me in Paradise" (Luke 23:43). In resurrection, He appears in His disciples' midst with the words, "Peace to you" (John 20:26). We have peace with God through our Lord Jesus Christ (Romans 5:1). We can know the peace of God, which surpasses all understanding, and we can know the God of peace (Philippians 4:7,9).

Given this incredible manifestation of God's peace in Christ, why would "the peace of God" not rule in our hearts (Colossians 3:15)? Why would we not be "at peace among (our)selves" (1 Thessalonians 5:13)? Why would we not "pursue righteousness faith, love and peace"? (2 Timothy 2:22). Why would we not be "peaceable, gentle, showing humility to all men"? (Titus 3:2). And why would we not be peacemakers and never be known as troublemakers?

The Great Peacemaker has made us the children of God. Let us walk through this new day, grounded in the gospel of peace, witnessing to it and ready to be peacemakers.

Day 93

Monday

The persecuted

*"Blessed are those who are persecuted for righteousness' sake,
For theirs is the kingdom of heaven."* (Matthew 5:10)

Persecution means to subject people to ill-treatment, often with their complete destruction in view. We see in the Acts of the Apostles that, once the Church was born and flourished, persecution began. The Lord Jesus told His disciples, "If they persecuted Me, they will also persecute you" (John 15:20). The religious authorities persecuted the apostles Peter and John, and then Stephen. The death of Stephen led to the great persecution in Acts 8. It was systematic, organised and led by a zealous Pharisee called Saul. He recalls in Acts 22:4, "I persecuted this Way to the death, binding and delivering into prisons both men and women."

In Acts 12 the state, under Herod, also persecutes the Church, killing James and arresting Peter. Throughout the history of the Church of Christ it has suffered persecution at the hands of religious and political powers. It is a history that continues to this day. May we always remember so many of our brethren who are hated, pursued, imprisoned, tortured and killed in so many parts of the world. They should always be in our hearts and prayers, and their faith should encourage us.

Persecution is founded on unrighteousness. The Saviour was hounded by the Pharisees, Levites, evidenced from the Parable of the Good Samaritan, and lawyers for doing good, with a thirst that was only satisfied by His death. But His sufferings revealed the heart of God in all its abundance of love and grace.

The persecution of the apostles served to demonstrate their utter faith and joy in God. Persecution scattered the Christians beyond Jerusalem and began an explosion of evangelism, prophesied by the Lord Jesus is Acts 1:8, which still burns brightly. Persecution led Saul to the feet of Jesus, and caused the Philippian jailer to ask Paul, "What must I do to be saved?".

The Kingdom of Heaven emphasises the earthy aspect of the Kingdom of God. In the promised millennial kingdom, righteousness will reign. The world, which is currently characterised by injustice, will be put to rights by the King of kings and Lord of lords. Under Christ's reign, the kingdom will belong to the lowly, to those who mourned, the meek, those who hungered and thirsted for righteousness, the merciful, the pure in heart, the peacemakers, and those who were persecuted for righteousness' sake – those who were hated in the world, driven from it, and "of whom the world was not worthy" (Hebrews 11:38). "Theirs is the kingdom of heaven."

As Christians we are already in the Kingdom of God spiritually. We recognise and live in the light of Christ's rule and authority in our hearts and fellowship. The kingdom also has in view rewards for our faithfulness to the Lord. Currently, the King is rejected, but returning. In the meantime, it is for us to manifest the gracious features the Lord Jesus spoke of in the Beatitudes. He was the perfect expression of holy lowliness, sorrow, meekness, righteousness, mercy, purity, peace and suffering. It is our calling to follow Him and express these beautiful features of Christ by the power of the Holy Spirit. Such fruitfulness glorifies the Father (John 15:8).

Day 94

Tuesday

Good soil

"*Behold, a sower went out to sow. And as he sowed, some seed fell ... on good ground and yielded a crop: some a hundredfold, some sixty, some thirty. He who has ears to hear, let him hear!*"

(Matthew 13:3-9)

In my last job I worked in conservation and attended many events. At one annual conference the subject was soil. I am a positive person, but I felt a whole day on soil would be testing. In the event, it was the most impressive secular conference I have ever attended. It made me understand why the Lord would base one of His most important parables on this vital subject.

The parable speaks about three problems which still occupy the finest minds in agriculture: hardness, erosion and weeds. The Lord tells the parable to outline how the word of God is received and understood. It has been used over and over again to preach the Gospel. But the conditions the Lord speaks about are also conditions which can affect the spiritual welfare of the people of God. Good soil can become hard, can erode and can be infertile.

The hardness of land prevents water from freely travelling into the soil to provide adequate irrigation. The word of God cannot fall, like the grain in John 12:24, to bear much fruit because the earth is not prepared to receive it. Our hearts can harden and become unreceptive to the word of God. We can become overfamiliar with ministry and cease to allow the word of God to flow daily, with refreshing, cleansing and sanctifying power, into our hearts. Erosion is a different problem. Heat and wind scorch the earth and drive away the topsoil, exposing lifeless rocks. Circumstances and forces which confront us in our lives either draw us into God's presence, or drive us away, embittering and robbing our hearts and spirits. Weeds choke the earth, wasting its resources and not allowing good things to grow. The Lord explains that the cares of the world deprive us of contentment, and the deceitfulness of riches absorbs our energies, leaving no room for spiritual growth.

I used to tell the story at a children's meeting about Mr Pipe and Mr Pot. I had two models to represent each character. I also had small cards with Bible verses written on them which I read and dropped behind the models. The verses fell into a pot which received the word of God and a pipe that did not. I explained to the children the importance of having a heart ready to receive Christ. But what the children did not know was that Mr Pipe was based on a real person. A baptised brother, breaking bread in a Christian fellowship, was charged with embezzlement and ended up in prison. A friend visited him and asked him what had gone wrong. He replied, "I was like a pipe: the word of God went straight through me, and I didn't allow it to touch my heart."

The Lord Jesus became like a grain of wheat falling into the ground and dying alone (John 12:24). In doing so He eternally secured His people. Through grace we have received Him into our hearts. His love for us never grows cold. May our hearts never be hardened, never be driven away and never allow the world, that hated Christ, to displace the Lord Jesus in our hearts. Let us allow "the word of Christ" to dwell in us richly (Colossians 3:16), abundantly yielding holy worship, joyous service and thankful witness.

Day 95

Wednesday

Twelve features of abundant life in Christ (1-6)

So it was, while they conversed and reasoned, that Jesus Himself drew near and went with them. (Luke 24:15)

In Luke 24 and Acts 1, as the Lord closes His ministry on earth, I think He outlines for us the foundation, progress and completion of the Christian life. I like to think of these as the 12 features of abundant life in Christ.

1. The resurrection of Jesus Christ "Why do you seek the living among the dead? He is not here, but is risen! Remember how He spoke to you when He was still in Galilee, saying, 'The Son of Man must be delivered into the hands of sinful men, and be crucified, and the third day rise again'" (Luke 24:5-7).

The resurrection is the proof of the finished work of redemption. By faith in Christ, we are eternally saved and walk in the newness of life.

2. The presence of Jesus Christ "So it was, while they conversed and reasoned, that Jesus Himself drew near and went with them" (v. 15).

There are two parts to the story of the journey to Emmaus. During the first part, the disciples didn't know it was Jesus who was with them. They only discovered it was Jesus as they ate a meal together in their home. But Jesus was with them throughout the whole of the journey, whether they understood it or not. He has promised never to leave or forsake us.

3. The challenge of faith "O foolish ones, and slow of heart to believe in all that the prophets have spoken! Ought not the

Christ to have suffered these things and to enter into His glory?" (vv. 25-26).

Faith is also a journey, and on it our faith can stumble, or it can shine. Our faith in Christ for salvation should encourage us not to foolishly doubt or be slow to trust Him, but to follow Him wisely and eagerly by believing and obeying His word.

4. The light of God's word "And beginning at Moses and all the Prophets, He expounded to them in all the Scriptures the things concerning Himself" (v. 27).

We don't read and meditate on the word of God to become experts in exposition, but to learn of Christ. The word of God teaches me how to worship, follow and serve the Saviour, and reveals the whole counsel of God.

5. Burning hearts "And they said to one another, 'Did not our heart burn within us while He talked with us on the road, and while He opened the Scriptures to us?'" (v. 32).

God speaks directly to our hearts, revealing the Person of Christ and generating a response of love in our spirits.

6. Energetic lives "So they rose up that very hour and returned to Jerusalem, and found the eleven and those who were with them gathered together, saying, 'The Lord is risen indeed'" (vv. 33-34).

Faith in Christ, the light of God's word, and enflamed hearts produce energetic and focussed service. To be continued…

Day 96

Thursday

Twelve features of abundant life in Christ (7-12)

And He led them out as far as Bethany, and He lifted up His hands and blessed them. (Luke 24:50)

7. Peaceful spirits "Now as they said these things, Jesus Himself stood in the midst of them, and said to them, 'Peace to you'" (v. 36).

Christ brings peace to our hearts. The disciples didn't begin to enjoy His peace until He showed them His hands and feet. Our peace in Christ is based upon the sacrifice of Christ. We should never lose sight of its reality and the perfect salvation it has secured.

8. Opened minds "And He opened their understanding that they might comprehend the Scriptures" (v. 45).

The Lord wants us to have burning hearts, and He also wants us to have spiritual minds that understand the word of God. In these ways, we are personally blessed and become a blessing to our fellow believers and to our neighbours. At the beginning of His ministry, the Lord demonstrated that God's word is central to the pathway of faith (Luke 4:4).

9. Empowered witness "And you are witnesses of these things. Behold, I send the Promise of My Father upon you; but tarry in the city of Jerusalem until you are endued with power from on high" (vv. 48-49).

Witnessing can be nerve-racking. It is important to remember we are not alone in this endeavour. The Lord stands with us, and the Spirit of God indwells us.

10. Constant blessing "And He led them out as far as Bethany, and He lifted up His hands and blessed them. Now it came to pass, while He blessed them, that He was parted from them and carried up into heaven" (vv. 50-51).

The last vision the disciples had of the Lord Jesus was of Him ascending into heaven, with His arms outstretched and the wounds on His hands visible, so that we would know His love, care and blessing are unceasing.

11. Joyful worship "And they worshipped Him, and returned to Jerusalem with great joy, and were continually in the temple praising and blessing God. Amen" (vv. 52-53).

Luke records that before the disciples began their witness to Christ at Pentecost, there was a period of joyous worship. Service should always be preceded by worship; it should always accompany worship, and it should always end in worship.

12. Certain hope "This same Jesus, who was taken up from you into heaven, will so come in like manner as you saw Him go into heaven" (Acts 1:11).

Just as angels announced the birth of the Saviour, so it was their privilege to announce the return of the Saviour and affirm in our hearts the hope we have in Christ: "This hope we have as an anchor of the soul, both sure and steadfast" (Hebrews 6:19).

"I have come that they may have life, and that they may have it more abundantly" (John 10:10).

Day 97

Friday

Ensuring we enjoy abundant life in Christ

Jesus cried with a loud voice, "Lazarus, come forth!" And he who had died came out bound hand and foot with graveclothes, and his face was wrapped with a cloth. Jesus said to them, "Loose him, and let him go." (John 11:43-44)

Therefore if the Son makes you free, you shall be free indeed. (John 8:36)

I knew a dear sister who, before she came to the Lord, was a chain-smoker. When she trusted the Lord, she never smoked another cigarette throughout the rest of her life. The Lord has the power to set us free from those things which can prevent us from enjoying the liberty we have in Christ. For this to happen, we need to exercise faith in Christ and allow His word to be our guide.

The name Lazarus is derived from Eleazar, a son of Aaron who was Moses' brother and Israel's first High Priest. His name means "God has helped". Of all the people the Lord Jesus helped, there was none in such an impossible state as Lazarus. Death had stripped him of a life in which he was loved by his family and by the Saviour. Sin and death separate us from God and all His blessings. Jesus came to conquer death and give us life "more abundantly" (John 10:10).

Not long after Jesus had said regarding Lazarus, "Loose him, and let him go", we read about the Saviour in the Garden of Gethsemane. When the soldiers arrived, Jesus asked them, "Whom are you seeking?" and they replied, "Jesus of Nazareth". Jesus simply said, "I am He" and they drew back and fell to the ground. Then Jesus allowed them to arrest and bind Him, whilst His disciples escaped. The Lord was not bound by the soldiers' ropes in Gethsemane or the nails at Calvary: He was bound by divine love. At Pentecost, Peter fearlessly declared the resurrection of Jesus Christ: "whom God raised up, having loosed the pains of death, because it was not possible that He should be held by it" (Acts 2:24). Christ's love is stronger than death.

There was no doubt Lazarus was alive, but He was bound hand and foot. Even his face was covered. The process of releasing him from his grave clothes required Lazarus to be still and his friends to patiently and gently remove what hindered his new life. In chapter 12, we find Lazarus in fellowship with the Lord. Afterwards, we see him witnessing to and suffering with the Lord (John 12:2,9-11).

The question we have to address is the impact our old life has on the enjoyment of our new life in Christ. The Saviour did not only give us life, but He also enables us to enjoy and express that life. Just as we came to the Saviour to receive life, we must abide in Him, who is our life, day by day. We need the stillness of His presence and power of His word to deal with all that would hinder the power and joy of Christian living. We need the fellowship and help of fellow Christians who love and care for us and whom we trust. Lazarus could not release himself. He was forced to be dependent. Dependency is not weakness; it is a human condition. We either rely on ourselves in an uncertain and fragile world, or we live by faith in a risen Christ. By being released, Lazarus did not become independent; he became free indeed.

Day 98

Saturday

Be anxious for nothing

Be anxious for nothing, but in everything by prayer and supplication, with thanksgiving, let your requests be made known to God; and the peace of God, which surpasses all understanding, will guard your hearts and minds through Christ Jesus.

(Philippians 4:6-7)

I think we have all had our fair share of anxiety over the past months—worries about health, employment, finances, family, fellowship, and living in a world of increasing uncertainty. How do we cope in such circumstances?

The apostles did not always cope well. Whilst the Lord was with them, they often struggled with His teaching and demonstrated feeble faith. But they were changed when the Lord ascended into heaven, and the Holy Spirit descended to indwell them and be with them. They were no longer afraid or hesitant, but full of victorious and bold faith which conquered adverse circumstances.

Paul illustrates this pattern of life in the final chapter of Philippians, against a background of imprisonment and isolation. Prison is designed to breed fear, uncertainty and overwhelming anxiety. But sometimes our imprisonment is not strong walls, bars and unfeeling guards. Our confinement is within us and created by the worries and fears that surround us.

So how was it that instead of the apostle's spirit being crushed, he lived in joyous liberty in the most oppressing circumstances? The church in Philippi sprang up, in part, by what God accomplished through the imprisonment of Paul and Silas in

Acts 16. Years later, from another prison Paul wrote to them about the life of Christ (1:21), the mind of Christ (2:5), the knowledge of Christ (3:10) and the strength of Christ (4:13). And he did this whilst demonstrating that his sufferings were his opportunities to manifest Christ. Paul and the apostles did not only turn the world upside down, but they also turned their experiences upside down: what should have destroyed them became their victory in Christ by the power of the Holy Spirit.

This begins, in verse 1 of chapter 4, with a Christ-filled spirit: "Stand fast in the Lord." Paul's faith rested utterly in Christ, and from this base everything was built. Paul had a helpful spirit: "Help these women" (v. 3). He was a problem-solver. It's not difficult to find a problem, or to cause one. It is far more challenging to find and implement solutions. And we should do this with a joyful spirit: "Rejoice in the Lord" (v. 4). The Philippian epistle is permeated by joy. Prisons were created to inflict despair and hopelessness. Paul overwhelmed the darkness of prison life with his joy in Christ. Recently, I spoke with a sister who is gravely ill. Her joyfulness, thankfulness and peacefulness in the midst of her pain and suffering lit up our conversation.

Prisons can be cruel places, but Paul had a gentle spirit: "Let your gentleness be known to all" (v. 5). They can be places where fear and loneliness reign. But Paul had a prayerful spirit. Prayer imparts a peaceful spirit as we experience "the peace of God" and the presence of the "God of peace" (vv. 7, 9). This leads to reflection and development of spiritual behaviour (vv. 8-9). There is little to comfort in prisons. But it did not rob Paul of his contented and generous spirit. He appreciated what others did for him: "You shared in my distress" and sought their blessing (vv. 11, 14, 19). Finally, Paul had a worshipping spirit: "Now to our God and Father be glory forever and ever. Amen" (v. 20). Prison could not prevent Paul's spirit soaring into the presence of God. In these ways the apostle teaches us how to escape the prison of anxiety by embracing the liberty of our life in Christ.

Day 99

Sunday

A man of sorrows

He is despised and rejected by men,
A Man of sorrows and acquainted with grief.
And we hid, as it were, our faces from Him;
He was despised, and we did not esteem Him.
Surely He has borne our griefs And carried our sorrows.

(Isaiah 53:3-4)

Every year thousands of people die because of age, disease, accident and crime. Numbers never describe the personal loss and heartbreak which death brings. This is especially felt when death comes suddenly and early in life.

In Isaiah 53 the Lord is described as "A Man of sorrows and acquainted with grief". Isaiah wrote prophetically of the Lord's person and work of redemption. He came into the world as the Sympathiser and the Saviour. God spoke to Moses in the book of Exodus about this,

> And the LORD said: "I have surely seen the oppression of My people who are in Egypt, and have heard their cry because of their taskmasters, for I know their sorrows. So I have come down to deliver them" (Exodus 3:7-8).

These verses explain that God felt in heaven what His people endured on earth; He sympathised. But He also promised to deliver; He saved. Christianity is about the Creator coming into His creation. The Lord Jesus used the simplest of illustrations to describe His profound ministry. In the Parable of the Good Samaritan, He comes to where we are. In the Parable of the Lost Sheep, the shepherd searches until He finds us. Jesus also came to Sychar's well to meet a lost woman, and to Jericho to meet a lost Zacchaeus. At Calvary, He came to sacrifice Himself for a lost world. His heart of love is revealed in His pain, suffering and death.

In her loss, Mary wept, broken-hearted at feet of Jesus. Jesus did not declare to Mary, "I am the resurrection and the life." Instead, He saw her tears and sorrow and felt her pain in His own heart, and He wept. The bystanders witnessed that moment: "See how He loved him!" (John 11:32-36).

One day, Jesus will take away tears, death, sorrow, crying and pain (Revelation 21:4). The Bible teaches us that, in the future, we will be gathered as one great company to be with the Lord, and be united by Him – so shall we ever be with the Lord (1 Thessalonians 4:15-18). We are to comfort each other with this hope. But that day is not today. Today is when Jesus empathises with us in our tears, our sorrow, our crying and pain. It is the day when He feels and shares in our broken heartedness. It is a love that comforts us in our loss and fills our hearts with hope. It is a love that sustains us through the bitterest of circumstances. It is also a love that makes us sensitive to the loss of others, encouraging us to always be compassionate, loving, tender-hearted and humble (1 Peter 3:8).

This is the love of Christ. It is a love that never fails (1 Corinthians 13:8).

Day 100

Monday

The disciple's Teacher: "Come to Me"

"Come to Me, all you who labour and are heavy laden, and I will give you rest. Take My yoke upon you and learn from Me, for I am gentle and lowly in heart, and you will find rest for your souls. For My yoke is easy and My burden is light."

(Matthew 11:28-30)

Matthew 11:28-30 is a passage that we often preach the gospel from and to which we turn for comfort when the stresses of life bear in upon us. I think, too, that in these verses, the Lord teaches us about the foundations of discipleship. Over the next few days, I want to reflect on His words.

A disciple is a learner who follows. It is not "remote learning" via the internet. Disciples learn by being in the company of their Teacher. Their discipleship is developed by listening, considering, observing, understanding and living in the good of what they have learned. The Lord Jesus speaks of us as "my disciples", and their characteristics include abiding in Christ's word – the light of God (John 8:31-32), being in God's family – the love of God (John 8:35) and by bearing much fruit – the life of God (John 15:8). One synonym of "disciple" is "adherent". This, in turn, is connected with the word "adhesive", meaning "sticking to". The secret of true discipleship is sticking close to the Saviour (John 15:5).

Let's start with the Lord's words, "Come to Me." John 1 gives us a great example of the first steps of discipleship: coming to Jesus. John the Baptist sees Jesus walking and says, "Behold the Lamb of God!" (v. 29). Two of John's own disciples heard his words and at that moment felt the compulsion to follow Jesus. We often think of Christ's call to follow Him, and this happened many times in the Gospels. But in John 1 we see the other side of discipleship – how seeing the Lord transforms our lives and compels us to want to follow him.

Interestingly, the Lord asked them what they wanted. Their first word to Jesus was "Teacher". They had only just heard the Lord speak for the first time, "What do you want?", but instinctively they submitted themselves to Him as their Teacher, and felt an immediate desire to be in His presence: "Where are you staying?" This is not the Lord asking them to follow, but them wanting to follow the Lord. It was the beginning of a life of "following". It was not a distant or secret following. No, this was a wholehearted commitment to closely follow the Saviour. They fundamentally understood the need to be close to their Teacher.

Jesus said, "Come and see." When the tabernacle and temple were completed in the Old Testament, the glory of God filled them, and neither Moses nor the priests could draw near. In John 1, the one who brought all things into being was walking in the world He had created. When two ordinary men followed Him, His first disciples, there was no distance or barrier, but an invitation to come close: "Come and see." They responded to what is in the Lord's heart towards all of us: "Come unto Me." It is an invitation to receive salvation and life. He never ceases to appeal to us to draw near to Him. The challenge is to daily discover and experience the light, love and life we have in our Lord Jesus Christ and to learn to follow and become like Him.

Day 101

Tuesday

The disciple's rest

"Come to Me, all you who labour and are heavy laden, and I will give you rest." (Matthew 11:28)

Discipleship begins by coming to Jesus. We have a tendency to concentrate on the cost of discipleship. This is a vital aspect of following Jesus. But it is not where we begin. Discipleship does not start with carrying burdens, but with our burdens being carried. The first thing we learn about Jesus Christ is His ability to carry. Isaiah 53:4 tells us, "He has borne our griefs and carried our sorrows." The Lord speaks in Luke 15:5-6 about the shepherd laying the sheep on his shoulders and carrying it home. Peter writes "who Himself bore our sins in His own body on the tree" (1 Peter 2:24). In 1 Peter 5:7 we are invited to cast "all your care upon Him, for He cares for you". This ministry of care did not stop at our salvation. It is lifelong. One of our greatest difficulties is learning to cast our care upon the Saviour and to rest in Him. It is a verse we love to quote, but rarely fully understand.

The Lord looked into Martha's heart (Luke 10:41) and said: "Martha, Martha, you are worried and troubled about many things." The Lord knew it wasn't just cooking Martha was concerned about. There were many burdens she carried in her heart, and I suspect most of these were burdens of others. How many burdens do we carry for ourselves, our family, our fellowship, our work and our health? The Lord encourages us to bear one another's burdens. But to do this most effectively we have to learn to have our cares carried by the Saviour. Remember the sense of liberty that rushed into your soul when you trusted

Jesus Christ. We found peace with God because the Saviour took our burden of sin and redeemed us. The power of true discipleship is to learn to unburden our souls in His presence and know there is not a weight that bears down upon us that He cannot carry.

When the Lord speaks of finding rest in Him, He is not speaking of inactivity. He is speaking of fulfilment. When Martha's sister, Mary, sat at the feet of Jesus, it was not in idleness. She was more alive at that moment than she had ever been in her life before. She drank in every word the Lord spoke, and she immediately understood the power of being in the presence of the Saviour.

"Heavy laden" means "heaped upon". It is in learning to "heap" our care upon the Lord that we discover His rest. In the Hastings' Bible Dictionary, J. Patrick describes this rest as "not the rest of inactivity but of the harmonious working of all the faculties and affections – of will, heart, imagination, conscience – because each has found in God the ideal sphere for its satisfaction and development." In other words, "For to me, to live is Christ" (Philippians 1:21).

Discipleship begins by learning to unburden ourselves of all that would hinder us from following the Saviour and from living in the liberty of "the Spirit of life in Christ Jesus" (Romans 8:2). We experience the peaceful harmony of body, soul, mind and spirit as we follow our Saviour and Lord in true discipleship and respond daily to His simple words, "You Follow Me" (John 21:22).

Day 102

Wednesday

The disciple's yoke

"Take My yoke upon you and learn from Me." (Matthew 11:29)

A yoke is a name given to a frame which harnesses two animals to work together. This is not the only description of a yoke, but it is the one which the Lord Jesus had in mind when He said: "Take My yoke upon you and learn from Me." He uses the yoke as a metaphor for His authority and our submission and obedience in discipleship. The way the Lord introduces "My yoke" is compelling. He doesn't force His yoke upon us; he invites us to take it willingly and walk in fellowship with Him.

He willingly took a yoke Himself. As the perfect Man in this world, He submitted Himself to the will of God the Father, and in holy submission "He humbled Himself and became obedient to the point of death, even the death of the cross." This yoke could not be shared; He bore its full weight. His sufferings led to glory and ultimately to the day when "at the name of Jesus every knee should bow, of those in heaven, and of those on earth, and of those under the earth, and that every tongue should confess that Jesus Christ is Lord, to the glory of God the Father" (Philippians 2:8 and 10-11).

We recognise His Lordship now. This is expressed in the yoke of discipleship and the learning from Christ which emerges from it. When a new ox is put to work to plough a field, it is placed beside an older and experienced animal within a yoke. In this way, the younger animal learns to follow and understand what to do and where to go. When we think of a disciple, we think of a follower. We tend to think of a leader in front and the follower behind. But this is not the only way to follow. If you met me in the small shopping centre near our house, and you asked me where I lived, I would say to you, "Follow me; I only live a few minutes away." How would you follow me? Would you walk behind? No, you would walk beside me and together we would walk to my home. You wouldn't know the way, but you would learn it by following side by side with the person who lives there. Through our verse this morning, we gain an understanding of discipleship that we so often overlook. We learn from being beside the Lord and we follow by being next to the One who will guide us all the way to His home.

The picture is a beautiful one, but how does it work? After Jacob wrestled with God, he limped for the rest of his life. Every step he took each day was a reminder of the day he met God. Discipleship is a step by step spiritual journey in which we are assured of the presence of the Lord by our side. There needs to be the time in our day when we come into His presence. There we listen to His word and respond in worship, thanksgiving, intercession and supplication. This communion with the Saviour leads us through the entirety of our lives in both the small and the most important decisions we make. The love of God is poured out in our hearts by the Holy Spirit (Romans 5:5), who demonstrates that we are the Lord's disciples by the love we have for each other. The Lord Jesus describes His Father as the vinedresser who stoops to ensure the life we have in Christ is seen in us through the fruit of the Holy Spirit (John 15:1). God has provided for us in every way to be effective disciples. The challenge is to live "by faith in the Son of God, who loved me and gave Himself for me" (Galatians 2:20) and who is always by our side (Matthew 28:20).

Day 103

Thursday

The disciple's transformation

"I am gentle and lowly in heart, and you will find rest for your souls. For My yoke is easy and My burden is light."

(Matthew 11:29-30)

Discipleship is a journey of transformation. One of the most powerful examples of transformation in the Bible is the story of the Philippian jailer in Acts 16. Paul and Silas, severely beaten, were handed over to the jailer. He placed them in the inner prison, fastening their feet in stocks. And that night, he appeared to have gone to bed without a thought for their welfare. But the earthquake which woke him brought him to the same men to ask the question, "What must I do to be saved?" The jailer trusted Christ as his Saviour, and this transformed his life. He took Paul and Silas into his own home, gave them first aid and fed them. The cruellest of men became the gentlest of men. The jailer had learned instantaneously to become Christlike.

Pride and self-interest should not characterise the Christian's life. Instead, Christ's gentleness and lowliness of heart should be seen in us. Gentleness is the characteristic of consideration towards others, with a tender and understanding heart, that seeks their blessing. And humility should clothe us (1 Peter 5:5). As we abide in Christ, these features of the fruit of the Spirit are produced. Gentleness is associated with meekness. It is a spiritual attitude of dependence upon God. There is an absence of struggling and a calm trust in God's strength and blessing. We see this in Peter when king Herod imprisoned him, in Acts 12. Herod intended to execute the apostle, but Peter was fast asleep, and an angel arrived to rescue him. The once self-confident disciple had grown in grace and rested in the Lord. Peter's letters reveal to us how he had heeded the Lord's words, "You follow Me", cast his care upon the Lord, and humbled himself under the mighty hand of God. He knew that the Lord would preserve him spirit, soul and body.

The Lord wants us to be at peace in all the circumstances of life. We discover the Lord's yoke of discipleship is "easy" or "kindly" because the Lord is beside us. And the burdens God asks us to bear are light in weight because He helps us to carry them. Meekness is not weakness; it is how God transmits His power through His people. We used to have a gas cooker which was getting old and was a little noisy and slow. The flames were high and you needed protection for your hands to lift pans off the hob. Recently we bought an induction cooker. You can't see any flames or glowing elements. Instead, by the silent, invisible power of electricity, the pans heat very quickly, and you can safely pick them up. The power of God is not flamboyant or ostentatious. It is seen in the gentle and lowly Person of Christ, the most powerful man who ever lived in this world. When we abide in Christ, His power flows through us. In the Old Testament, Isaiah writes,

> For thus says the High and Lofty One
> Who inhabits eternity, whose name is Holy:
> "I dwell in the high and holy place,
> With him who has a contrite and humble spirit"
> (Isaiah 57:15).

As we follow the Lord as our Teacher, as we find our fulfilment by resting in Him, and as we take His yoke upon us, we are transformed into His likeness and become Christians who are "strong in the Lord and in the power of His might" (Ephesians 6:10).

Day 104

Friday

Psalm 1

Blessed is the man... *(Psalm 1:1)*

The Psalms is the book in the Bible with the most verses. The first psalm starts with words addressed to our individual hearts, "Blessed is the man." The last, Psalm 150, ends with the words, "Let everything that has breath praise the LORD. Praise the LORD!" In Psalm 1, we are given a real sense of God's desire to bless us individually. In Psalm 150:6, the writer places in our hearts the wonder of the day when the whole of creation will "Praise the LORD!" It is incredible that God, who is the centre of that explosion of praise, touches our hearts one by one. God does not simply view us as a countless multitude praising Him. He sees every individual whom He has embraced within His love. He knows every one of His children by name.

Interestingly, Psalm 1 begins by associating our blessing with what we should not do. Verse 1 succinctly describes a dangerous downward journey. It starts by walking in the company of the ungodly. It leads down sinful paths to a destination away from God. It stops outside the house of the scornful. And, finally, it steps inside to sit down in the company of those in opposition to God. The Psalmist describes what the Lord later taught in the parables of the Prodigal Son and the Good Samaritan.

This downward journey is the opposite of the journey on the road to Emmaus. On that journey the disciples walked with the Saviour. They stood outside their house and compelled the Lord to come in and abide with them. Then they sat in fellowship with the risen Saviour.

The Psalmist describes the delight God's children find in His living word and the joyful commitment by which it is assimilated into their lives: "His delight is in the law of the LORD" (v. 2). In John 15, the Lord encourages us to abide in Him and bear spiritual fruit in our lives. Paul lists the characteristics of the fruit of the Spirit in Galatians 5:22-23: "The fruit of the Spirit is love, joy, peace, longsuffering, kindness, goodness, faithfulness, gentleness, self-control." In Psalm 1:3, we are likened to "a tree planted by the rivers (streams) of water, that brings forth its fruit in its season". The Psalmist is illustrating our individual fellowship with God through His word. The streams of water have their source in God. We see the river of life in Revelation 22:1 has its source in "the throne of God and of the Lamb". And the Tree of Life and the twelve fruits it bears continually throughout the year (v. 2) are also described. Our spiritual fruitfulness is dependent on abiding in the living Christ and His living word. Water is used as an illustration of the word of God (Ephesians 5:26). We develop fruitful lives by reading, meditating, trusting, obeying and allowing the word of Christ to dwell in us richly (Colossians 3:16); we prosper in God's sight (Psalm 1:3).

The Psalmist ends with a further warning about where the path of the ungodly ends. We are accountable to God for the lives we live. We cannot stand based on what we are or what we can do. Peter fell into that trap, and Satan sought to sift Him as wheat to be driven away and lost (v. 4). But the Lord prayed for Peter and he discovered his righteousness was in Christ. He is also our righteousness; all our resources are found in Him, and we can walk with God (v. 6a).

Day 105

Saturday

Gold, silver and precious stones

Now if anyone builds on this foundation with gold, silver, precious stones.   *(1 Corinthians 3:12)*

In the third chapter of 1 Corinthians Paul describes how he and Apollos were involved in the service of God. He speaks about how he had planted, Apollos watered, but God gave the increase. It is good to see Paul recognising Apollos' service and demonstrating how their work was harmonised and used by God to bring an increase in the Gospel and the building up of the people of God. Paul gives God the glory because He is the one who alone gives this increase. Paul had laid a foundation in Christ, but he recognises everything is done under the hand of God, "For we are God's fellow workers; you are God's field, you are God's building" (v. 9). Sometimes we can become detached from this truth and start acting as though the service which God graciously involves us in belongs to us. And we can cease to value the contribution and gift of others. The Lord Jesus always encouraged His disciples to work together in fellowship and understand they were sent by Him, and He would work with them (Mark 16:20). We have different gifts and abilities, and it is a joyous experience when these are blended together for the glory of God.

I baked my first cake last week under the skilled eye of June. I was amazed at how the different ingredients can be blended together to create something remarkable. But it was all done under the direction of one person. God takes His people, who can be so diverse, and blends us into a fellowship of life, love and light. At the same time, He works in each of our hearts, making us more Christlike and uniting us in His love. It is amazing, when visiting the people of God in another country with significant differences of language and culture, how we immediately find joyful fellowship with other Christians because we are one in Christ Jesus.

Paul is primarily thinking of evangelism and the teaching of the doctrines of faith founded in Christ. But we need to heed Paul's challenge about how we build on this foundation. His list of gold, silver, precious stones, wood, hay, straw, is split between what the fire refines or proves and what it destroys; what is precious and what perishes; what has eternal value and what will vanish. The gold, silver and precious stones have always reminded me of three vital aspects of the Christian life. First, Gold. This was used in the Tabernacle and the Temple, where God was present and was worshipped. We see this in the Mercy Seat (Exodus 25:17) and in His people's righteousness represented in the gold-covered boards (Exodus 26:29) which formed the Tabernacle. Our lives should be a response of worship to God. Second, Silver. This is connected with redemption and the work of Christ. The gold-covered boards were set on two silver bases (Exodus 26:19). This is a wonderful reminder that we stand in Christ and the power of His death and resurrection. Finally, God's people and their preciousness was represented by the twelve precious stones on the breastplate which was carried over the High Priest Aaron's heart (Exodus 28:15-30). Now our life is hidden with Christ in God (Colossians 3:3). We are in the heart of the Saviour who is our Great High Priest (Hebrews 4:14). So, how should I build? By worshipping the Father, witnessing to Christ, and working by the Holy Spirit of God to fulfil Christ's command to love, serve and value my brothers and sisters in Christ.

About the Author

Gordon Kell has been involved in Christian ministry for over fifty years. Apart from a period of five years in full-time Christian service, this has always been in a "tentmaking" capacity. With his wife, June, their Christian ministry has included young peoples' work, camps, Christian holidays, young married couples' weekends, and conferences throughout the UK and occasionally in Europe. Until recently, Gordon's written ministry was linked with his long involvement in radio Bible teaching. Gordon and June have one daughter, three granddaughters and a grandson, and live in Northern Lincolnshire, not far from the birthplace of John Wesley who once said, "Let your words be the genuine picture of your heart."

Gordon commands a wide respect for "rightly handling the word of truth" (2 Timothy 2:15), combining awareness of its depth with succinctness and a personable style.

www.ingramcontent.com/pod-product-compliance
Lightning Source LLC
Chambersburg PA
CBHW070142100426

42743CB00013B/2803